Library of Congress Cataloging-in-Publication Data

LCCN 2010906124
ISBN 1451599145
EAN-13 9781451599145

D'Amico, James V.
    The affluenza antidote: How wealthy families can raise grounded children in an age of apathy and
    entitlement / James V. D'Amico

Cover design by Melanie A. Watson

For more information about The Affluenza Antidote, to contact the author, or to obtain additional
copies, visit www.AffluenzaAntidote.com.

THE

AFFLUENZA
ANTIDOTE

How Wealthy Families
Can Raise Grounded Children
in an Age of Apathy and Entitlement

James V. D'Amico
2010

This book is dedicated to my wife, Renee, with whom I have shared more than four wonderful decades. My primary advocate throughout this literary journey, she fully appreciates my strong feelings on these topics. Most important, she has helped me fine-tune my values, parenting approaches and many of the thoughts on societal changes I have expressed here. For this manuscript, Renee also has provided a valuable mother's perspective.

In addition, I dedicate this book to my mother, Ann Maggio. Widowed at age 41, she nevertheless managed to provide and maintain our family's structure and value system – which became the foundation for my own childrearing efforts.

Acknowledgments

The following deserve special recognition:

■ Our interviewee families, who – in agreeing to speak candidly for this book about sensitive but vital issues – provide hope, humor and guidance for other families of wealth. (In keeping with our promise, names and other details that might identify them have been changed to protect their privacy.) May the courage they have shown – to parent with strength, constancy and love, rather than succumb to cultural pressures to spoil their children – inspire future generations of parents.

■ My collaborator, Rose Benz Ericson, for her assistance in interviewing families, conducting research, drafting and editing this manuscript, and managing the publication process.

■ Those colleagues and friends, particularly estate attorney Bob Kessler, who introduced us to interviewee families.

■ The researchers, social scientists, educators, psychologists and writers whose study of parenting and wealth issues help provide a basis for this book.

■ My former clients, who have inspired me with their philanthropy and their enthusiasm for this project. In particular, I thank Joan and Harold Feinbloom, former owners of Champion Products Inc. and founders of Genesee Valley Trust Company. Joan and Harold allowed me to witness their brand of social responsibility as a dynamic intergenerational legacy.

■ My four children – Lance, Clifford, Allyson and Jaime – and their spouses – Katherine, Kelley, Doug and Kevin. Seeing our most cherished values come to life in them and in our grandchildren is the greatest gift any parent can receive.

Author's Note

Not-for-profit organizations play a crucial role in supporting our communities and providing families with opportunities to teach their children civic involvement.

In appreciation for those priceless contributions, a portion of the proceeds of sales of this book will be donated to select charities.

– *James V. D'Amico, June 2010*

Contents

Acknowledgments .... *vii*

Author's Note .... *vii*

Part I 11

   Introduction. Money Makes Life Easier – Or Does It? 13

   Chapter 1. What's Happened to Values? 21

      Changes in Family Structure...................................... 22

      Media and a Culture of Consumption 25

      Technology 25

      Failing Educational Systems 26

      Breakdown of Communities 26

      Dwindling Job Opportunities 27

      The Family Firm's Struggle for Longevity 27

   Chapter 2. Why Affluent Children Face Greater Risks 29

Part II 37

   Chapter 3. Building Resistance to Affluenza........................ 39

   Chapter 4. The Sacred Ritual of the Family Dinner 45

   Chapter 5. Instilling a Work Ethic and Respect for Money.............. 51

   Chapter 6. Cherishing Old-Fashioned Fun 63

   Chapter 7. Vacations and Extended Family.......................... 71

   Chapter 8. Modeling Philanthropy and Volunteerism................. 79

   Chapter 9. The Role of Religious Involvement 89

   Chapter 10. Shifting Attitudes About Education 95

   Chapter 11. The Family Business: A Blessing or a Curse?............. 109

Part III.. 119

   Conclusion. Can We Reverse Course?............................. 121

References 127

About the Author 133

Part I

Introduction
Money Makes Life Easier – Or Does It?

O nce upon a time, there lived a boy raised on hard work, honesty, loyalty, generosity and the love of family. In his traditional Italian household on Long Island, life revolved around family meals, neighborhood, school and church.

Money was tight, and the boy was eager to begin contributing. First he delivered newspapers, then took a job in a bakery. At 16, he began working as a lifeguard. When his father died soon after, finances became even tighter. Extra money would make life so much easier, he thought.

When getting to work required a car, the teenage boy bought a 10-year-old model for $35. He didn't consider asking his mother for $250 for insurance. If only he had more money, he believed, life would be easier.

An elite private college was out of the question, so he pursued his degree at a public university. His mother helped with some expenses, but he paid most of his bills using scholarships and earnings from high school and college jobs. Still, he thought, more money would be welcome.

At age 21, he married his high school sweetheart, whose family he'd known since Little League days. His wife's income was too small to sustain them in their own place, so they lived with her father during the young man's final year of college. Early on – and with little money – they started a family.

Our fellow pursued a career in trust banking, which introduced him to estate and investment work. For the first time, he began to see inside the lives of very wealthy people – older folks who exhibited salt-of-the-earth characteristics, the kind with which he had grown up. They were honest, hardworking and generous, devoted to their employees, the community and society. Money indeed had given them an ample array of comforts and opportunities, but they remained reliable and unpretentious. They were what authors Thomas Stanley and William Danko would later dub "the millionaires next door."

The boy, now grown to a man, assisted clients in transferring their hard-earned fortunes to their adult children, who would live lives of ease, pursuing fascinating interests and helping improve the world. Our fellow thought: How happy and engaged they must be! How comfortable! How loving and loyal!

Except – they weren't. Extra money – the very thing that our young man thought would enhance people's lives – was doing just the opposite, breeding unhappiness and maladjustment. Why were so many well-meaning parents with solid value systems ending up with children so debilitated by "affluenza"?

A Startling Realization

I was that boy. And this is what I saw:

■ Parents who had worked long hours and made great sacrifices to build a thriving family business, only to find they couldn't confidently leave the business in the hands of their unmotivated, ill-prepared children.

■ Adult children too often squandering their parents' carefully amassed fortunes on lavish living, gambling, fast cars, excessive alcohol and illegal drugs.

■ Acrimonious divorces leaving young children's lives torn apart and the family's hard-won resources claimed or diluted by spiteful ex-spouses.

■ Grandchildren used as pawns in the war between wealthy parents and their adult children – "Give me the money to pay my gambling debts, or your grandchildren won't visit this Christmas."

Initially, these bitter scenarios shocked me. But over the next 35 years, as my career led me to advise thousands of wealthy families, I came to realize that ugly circumstances like these were actually quite common. The more I learned of the intimate details of these families' lifestyles and finances, the more remarkable seemed the contrast between their lives and my own early years.

I saw that being blessed with vast material resources did not bring the younger generations lives of contentment, purpose, wisdom or generosity. Adult children who had every opportunity to continue their parents' legacy of hard work, innovation, job creation, civic involvement and philanthropy instead succumbed to chronic affluenza. They behaved like spoiled brats – materialistic, apathetic, lazy and entitled. Worst of all, they were raising their own children with virtually none of the values that had made their parents' generation a great one.

Spiraling Downward

But the problem goes beyond those few thousand families. Entire generations are now growing up fully absorbed with their own wants and oblivious to the greater needs around them. This self-centeredness masks a profound unhappiness and emptiness that money cannot ease or fill.

More and more, I see children raised in luxurious houses with their own rooms, televisions and computers – but little time and tough love from their career-obsessed parents. Because their families employ household help, few of these children learn to pitch in or take responsibility for themselves. They squander their rich educational opportunities by skipping classes, starting fights, mouthing off to teachers or simply failing to engage. Their parents, uncertain of what to do, defend them or ignore the problem.

Today's affluent teens are less likely to mow lawns or flip burgers than to receive shiny new cars as birthday gifts. Later many will damage those cars – often because they've been drinking, using drugs or otherwise behaving irresponsibly. But their parents will buy their way out of punishment – and might even reward them with replacement cars.

These children of privilege attend private colleges on their parents' dime – maybe graduating in four years, maybe not. They're powerfully drawn to high-risk activity and questionable friendships. A few will get into serious legal trouble – and their parents will hire attorneys to keep them out of jail. Many more will drift through the higher-education experience, failing to reap its benefits.

Eventually, some will go to work in the family's business, causing hard feelings among the long-term employees and dragging down company performance. Or they will drift from job to job, city to city, relying on subsidies from their parents. They may marry one, two, three times – with each union ending in a damaging divorce.

How have we arrived at such a state of family and societal deterioration? Has so much really changed in just my lifetime? How did my wife and I – the naïve, unprepared and undercapitalized new parents that we were – manage to raise four civil human beings who work hard, associate with people of high character, and contribute to society? We made mistakes, of course, and learned a lot the hard way. Still we wondered: How could we, with our middle-class backgrounds and resources, do what others with far more advantages could not?

I began to realize that I wasn't the only one asking these questions. For more than 10 years, I had written a regular column in a local business newspaper on matters concerning wealth management. Each time my topic addressed the complexities of transmitting values to heirs, or managing the tricky dynamics of a family business, reader response was swift and poignant.

Wealthy parents themselves were wondering: How can we prevent our family's money from ruining our children's lives? Can we enjoy our hard-earned wealth, or must we conceal it from our children? How can we teach our offspring to pursue meaningful employment when we have enough assets to bankroll them for life? Will sending our children to private schools doom them to immersion in snobbery? How do we ensure that our children develop an appreciation of money and compassion for the less fortunate?

One Family's Story

As I've said, my wife and I were young and had no particular insights into parenting. As most parents do, we drew on our own backgrounds to forge principles as we went along. I do remember a few early ideas we had – that we'd be "renting" children for a finite period and preparing them to seek their own destiny, and that if we screwed it up, we'd get no second chances.

Many factors combine to generate a successful child, or a troubled one. Our children benefited from living in one community for 17 years. Glens Falls, New York, is a modest place with little conspicuous consumption. Like most of our friends, we enjoyed a comfortable middle-class income. We were fortunate to live in the beautiful Adirondack Mountains, where nature provided us with countless opportunities for free recreation outdoors. We hiked regularly on weekends, always bringing a picnic lunch.

During the week, we ate home-cooked meals together most evenings. My wife and I coached Little League baseball and softball, and our children developed deep friendships at school and in the neighborhood. Entertaining meant playing cards over potluck at another family's home while our collected children played together.

When I was offered a job an hour away in Albany, I asked whether our family should move closer to my new opportunity. We took a vote – which I lost, 5 to 1. Staying in Glens Falls allowed our family to continue nourishing our roots, while I commuted an hour each way. Later we were transferred to Buffalo, but only after each of our children had had the opportunity to develop within an intact family and to experience the benefits of a cohesive community life.

In those years, common sense trumped status-seeking. When our children reached driving age, we didn't buy them cars; we made vehicles available or carpooled.

Two of our children were accepted at boarding schools and made the decision to attend. The other two, given the same choice, opted to remain home and attend public high schools. To cover boarding-school costs, my wife took a part-time job, our children obtained partial scholarships and student loans, and we secured a second mortgage.

When college decisions rolled around, we told our children that we would underwrite only so much. For every dollar of debt we took on, they would have to secure an equivalent amount. They used summer earnings toward living expenses, which we supplemented. Despite the challenges they would face in raising significant funds, all four chose private colleges.

At one point, our family was paying three tuition bills simultaneously. The two who went on to graduate school paid their own way.

Gratefully, I can say today that all four are raising wonderful families and enjoying fulfilling careers. My wife and I did our best most of the time – and we also benefited from good luck.

Our oldest is 40 and lives in California with his wife and three children, ages 10, 8 and 5. As a teen, he lifeguarded in a state park. He attended Deerfield Academy, Dartmouth College and New York University School of Law. At Deerfield, he was exposed to mega-wealthy students, some of whom were well-adjusted, interesting and generous, while others appeared troubled and isolated, perhaps suggesting greater problems at home. Exposure to this diverse student body has served our son well as an adult. Today he is general counsel at a publicly traded West Coast company.

Our second son is 39 and lives in Tampa with his wife and 8-year-old son. During high school, he worked as a laborer in a state park. Upon graduation from Denison University, my wife gave him two weeks to relax at home, after which he was expected to find a job. At the end of two weeks – much to his surprise and chagrin – she handed him a suitcase, a plane ticket to Orlando, Florida, and the phone number of a niece who had arranged a job interview and would provide him a temporary place to live. Our son landed the job and stayed with that company for 17 years. Recently, he formed a consultancy focused on energy price competitiveness and efficiency.

Our older daughter is 38 and lives in Chicago with her husband and three children, ages 12 through 9. As a teen, she also worked as a state park lifeguard. After prep school at Suffield Academy, she also attended Denison and ended up marrying her brother's roommate. She is very active in her community and organizes a charity toy giveaway every Christmas, an important tradition in her family. Recently she participated in a run to benefit breast cancer research.

Our youngest is 34 and lives in Florida with her husband and two children, ages 3 and 1. She graduated from Cornell University and then earned a master's degree in business from the University of Central Florida, where she works in the executive MBA program. A competitive runner, she recently completed the New York City Marathon.

Our extended family vacations together regularly so that our children, their spouses and our nine grandchildren can build meaningful connections. We also seek opportunities to expose the grandchildren to cultural diversity. We have stayed in rented houses in South Carolina, Florida, Jamaica and the Dominican Republic. Next up is Lake Tahoe, California.

On our 60th birthdays recently, our children gave my wife and me a plaque with text they had composed themselves, highlighting some of the principles and values we hold dear. The plaque reads, in part:

> *Love your kids fiercely.*
> *Never take family for granted.*
> *Remain young at heart.*
> *Work hard and smart and you can make a better life for yourself.*
> *Be involved in your kids' activities and lives.*
> *Share special events as a family.*
> *Stand up for what you believe in.*
> *There is such a thing as happily ever after.*

With that gift, our children made it clear that the messages we had attempted to weave into our parenting had hit their mark.

In Search of Role Models

Reared by common-sense folks ourselves, my wife and I and most of our friends didn't question the wisdom of going to work every day, saving money, spending carefully, teaching our children to respect authority, and giving back to the community. While unknown and uncontrollable factors can derail any child, even in the most diligent families, it seems no secret that sticking to these and similar values should be crucial in raising well-rounded children.

So why then did the children of so many wealthy clients seem to go wrong? Why didn't these values take root in them? Was excess money the sole cause of affluenza, or did other factors contribute?

Time and again, I have shuddered to think of how much society suffers when those who are given ample assets do not commit themselves to the welfare of future generations. If they do not do it, then who will?

To be sure, there's nothing new or unusual about wealthy children abusing their privilege. The Kennedys have been notorious for perpetuating the stereotype, as has Tony Marshall, convicted of stealing from his dying mother, socialite Brooke Astor. Closer to home, we've all known a few trust-fund babies whose lavish living, self-absorption, apathy, recklessness and unhappiness are legion.

But how many wealthy parents do we know who *are* raising their children to be the well-grounded, disciplined, generous citizens that our society so badly needs? These families may be in short supply, and – because they tend to live and work quietly, shunning high-profile exploits – we don't often hear of them.

Consider this: What if we could get to know them? Could we pinpoint what they're doing right? Could we identify the elements that create an environment where children have better odds of growing to their full potential, motivated to work hard, to improve the world, and to raise their own successful children? Would knowing something about the parenting styles and attitudes of these folks guide and inspire other parents of wealth to do a better job of immunizing their children against affluenza?

Chapter 1
What's Happened to Values?

T oday's children grow up with different values than yesterday's children did.

Notions that served previous generations well – self-reliance, thrift, honest labor, integrity, family stability, marital commitment, respect for others, religious affiliation and connection to community – have become quaint or irrelevant for much of the modern American population.

Many of our parents and grandparents struggled to survive financially, particularly during the Great Depression. Some were immigrants who suffered great hardship as they journeyed to this country, battling starvation and illness, and enduring the deaths of or separation from loved ones. Those who managed to thrive in the United States often did so because they labored from dawn to dusk on farms, or put in 14-hour days in factories or building their own businesses.

Rather than perpetuate these core traditions, however, many of today's families are floundering. Typically, we see:

▨ Working parents who are too stressed to teach delayed gratification and instead aim to satisfy their children's media-driven appetites for consumer goods.

▨ Children of divorced parents who are disciplined one way by Mom and another way by Dad – or perhaps not disciplined at all.

▨ Excessive exposure to boorish or reckless celebrities and sports figures who have gotten rich without working regular jobs and refuse to accept the responsibility to act as positive role models.

■ The decline of community standards, as neighbors, faith communities, schools and extended families lose their influence in childrearing.

■ Dramatic increases in depression – as high as tenfold – particularly among teens.

■ Lax enforcement at home that produces children who fear no consequences for disruptive behavior in school or criminal behavior on the streets. A generation ago, teachers could count on parents to back up their disciplinary actions. But schools today more often fear lawsuits by parents who refuse to believe that Junior deserves a failing grade or punishment for cheating on a test or threatening a teacher. How have we reached the stage where shootings like those at Columbine High School and Virginia Tech have become, if still tragic, almost inevitable?

Let's look more closely at some key factors contributing to the moral decline of modern society.

Changes in Family Structure

Dual-Income Families Become the Norm

In many ways, today's parents face more pressures than they did a generation ago. In 60 percent of American families, both parents work, government figures show – up from some 30 percent in 1975.

In dual-income families, children are not supervised as closely, nor do they experience as much unstructured face time with parents and siblings as we did a decade ago. According to the Peace Parenting Project, the average American child communicates with his or her parents a mere 12.5 minutes each day.

Parents who work long hours or travel for business frequently try to compensate by indulging their children too much, hoping that the latest computer game will serve as an adequate proxy for parental time and attention. This shortage of family time leaves many children feeling isolated and adrift, and their insecure parents feeling guilty and worn out. In their zeal to be popular with their children, many parents resist saying "no" to their children or holding them accountable for unacceptable behavior.

Decline of Family Dinnertime

American mothers have long fulfilled the role of meal preparer, an image immortalized by television's June Cleaver. In the last few decades, however, the fast-food and takeout culture has nearly obliterated the home-cooked family meal, a once-sacred institution.

"Food comes so easily to us now that we have lost a sense of its significance," says anthropologist Robin Fox. "When we had to grow the corn and fight off predators, meals included a serving of gratitude. ... Fast food has killed this. We have reduced eating to sitting alone and shoveling it in."

Is it any wonder that parents don't enforce family mealtimes? They come home from work drained, only to get back in the car to shuttle their children to music lessons, sports practices and school activities. The decline of the old-fashioned family dinner also has contributed to childhood obesity and nutrition-related diseases like diabetes.

> "In 1970, Americans spent about $6 billion on fast food; in 2000, they spent more than $110 billion. ... Americans now spend more money on fast food than on higher education, personal computers, computer software or new cars. They spend more on fast food than on movies, books, magazines, newspapers, videos and recorded music – combined."
>
> – Eric Schlosser, author, Fast Food Nation

As well, children who don't eat dinner with their families miss out on vital civilizing activities – helping prepare the meal, conversing with their siblings and parents, staying at the table until the meal is finished, and participating in the cleanup.

The Overscheduling and Overprotection of Children

In an era when parents are ever more concerned about crime and "bad influences," children enjoy less unstructured time to play outside, to discover nature, to play pickup sports or to ride bicycles. In an effort to minimize liability, municipalities, schools – even families – discourage free play outdoors.

Parents who skinned their knees on the playground of hard knocks often insist on shielding their children from the vital lessons that should naturally spring from everyday life. Sheltered children fail to learn to handle disappointment and frustration. They lack opportunities for sharing, taking turns or coping with bullying. Protected from the pain of making a mistake or losing a game, these children may not learn what it means to work hard, to aim for one's personal best and to accept disappointment gracefully.

Divorce

Only 63 percent of American children grow up with both biological parents – the lowest figure in the Western world. A 2005 report by the National Marriage Project found that, in 2003, 44 percent of custodial mothers and 56 percent of custodial fathers were either separated or divorced. Every year, author James Robbins reports, more than one million American children see their parents divorce.

Underlying those statistics are legions of guilt-ridden parents who struggle to compensate for their failure to keep the family together. And step-parenting raises particular challenges, as defiant children often refuse to accept the authority of the new spouse.

Mobility and Isolation

Research shows that the average American family moves to a different home every five years. At similar intervals, the average worker changes jobs.

All that mobility comes at a cost to families and communities. More and more, children are pulled away from friends and forced to start over in new schools and neighborhoods where, as outsiders, they're vulnerable to loneliness and bullying.

When families move – by choice, or forced by a job loss – children often end up thousands of miles from their grandparents, aunts, uncles and cousins – and the love, permanence and sense of identity that extended families provide.

Media and a Culture of Consumption

Before access to television and the Internet became ubiquitous in suburbia, young people had less opportunity to obsess over the goodies that other children enjoyed. Advertising reminds us, hundreds or thousands of times a day, what we "deserve," what we "must" have and how we must not "be left behind."

Increasingly, Americans see themselves primarily as consumers – and those who sell products and experiences have been very successful in convincing us that we want and need more. Seduced by a blurring of the line between needs and wants, and egged on by easy credit, many have become dangerously overextended, pushing credit-card defaults to an all-time high.

Consider trends in home sizes. While American families have gotten smaller, our houses have expanded. From 1950 to 2004, the size of the average new single-family home increased by nearly 140 percent, from 983 square feet to 2,349. But the soaring incidence of mortgage foreclosures and short sales provides evidence that many buyers' desires were grander than their ability to honor their financial commitments.

And where is Americans' emphasis on consumption more apparent than in our expanding waistlines? Government figures show that 73 percent of American adults in 2005-06 were overweight, obese or extremely obese – up from 59 percent for the 1988-94 period. Among the adolescent population, three times as many are overweight today as were in 1999.

Technology

Technology has taken over, bringing with it particularly virulent strains of affluenza. Children who stay inside all day in front of a screen typically expect the world to entertain them. Apathetic, they fail to develop social skills. They miss out on the joy of stretching their imaginations and discovering the world's enormity and diversity. Estranged from the natural world, they're at risk for obesity, hyperactivity, depression, violence, and abuse of alcohol and drugs.

Failing Educational Systems

Education costs more than ever, and yet schools are failing to accomplish what they did so well a generation or two ago.

Violence is on the rise. Parents are quicker to defend their children's boorish behavior than to support teachers' authority. Those who claim to be trumpeting individual rights challenge the recitation of the Pledge of Allegiance in classrooms, citing the unconstitutionality of the phrase "one nation under God." If we are not one nation under God, are we one nation under no god?

More Americans are graduating from college ill-equipped to work, even as the competition from highly educated, hardworking immigrants intensifies.

Breakdown of Communities

Communities have become far more fragmented. Frequent family moves thwart children's need to establish roots, and neighbors remain strangers rather than provide the supportive network that society once thrived on. Apathy, drug use and violence often fill the vacuum.

Membership in faith communities and civic organizations has dropped, depleting society of legions of volunteer workers and the vitality that togetherness generates.

In his landmark book, "Bowling Alone," researcher Robert D. Putnam examined a variety of civic-engagement indicators and found that fewer people are attending religious services, running for public office, attending meetings, participating in clubs, entertaining friends at home, donating money, working on community projects or giving blood.

And perhaps it's that loss of community that's driving up rates of unhappiness. Psychologist Martin Seligman found that depression rates have increased tenfold over the last generation. He and others suggest that isolation and boredom – two things that money *can* buy, quite effectively – may be significant contributors to the malaise.

Even more chilling is the increasing incidence of mass violence, suggesting that disrespect for human life has grown to epidemic levels.

Dwindling Job Opportunities

The nation's economic difficulties, coupled with growing competition from bright, eager foreigners, have shrunk the pool of meaningful job opportunities for everyone, but especially young people.

At the same time, young adults are less prepared to enter the job market. Parents, fearful of allowing their children to face the struggle that is part of life, provide far too many subsidies – thereby preventing the children from learning economic self-sufficiency, character and resilience.

The Family Firm's Struggle for Longevity

Raising affluenza-stricken children who yearn more for flashy cars than for building or expanding successful businesses weakens our economy in additional ways.

Only one-third of family firms survive into the second generation, the *Family Business Review* reports, and 12 percent survive into the third. Further, just 3 percent make it to the fourth generation or beyond.

Too often, those who inherit successful businesses seem to lack the passion and commitment that drove their parents – and which now drive their competitors. Could the tendency of wealthy parents to make their children's lives *too comfortable* contribute to a lack of motivation and achievement in the younger generation?

"(Rich kids) grow up in (what I call) 'enriched deprivation.' They have so much that everything becomes meaningless. ... They feel entitled to luxury and come to expect it. ... These kids become weak, jaded and ungrateful. ... They not only lack a sense of self-esteem, they lack a sense of self. They often become vulnerable to the (trap of) unbridled pleasure, since they have the time and money to pursue it."

– Dan Baker, author, What Happy People Know

Chapter 2
Why Affluent Children
Face Greater Risks

Recent economic woes notwithstanding, Americans are wealthy people. More than 9 million households were worth $1 million in 2007. While that figure declined during 2008, the fact remains that many, many families are raising children in far more luxurious circumstances than they or their grandparents experienced.

Our buying power has more than doubled since the 1950s, writes Gary W. Buffone, psychologist and author. In 2003, Americans owned twice as many cars as in 1975, ate out twice as often, and enjoyed a growing array of appliances, computers and technological toys.

> *"The problem with money ... is that it sets up its own paradox: Hard work may yield it, but growing up with it often discourages hard work."*
>
> – Jennifer Senior, writer,
> Rich Kid Syndrome, New York Magazine

But where is that affluence getting us? *New York Times* columnist David Brooks wrote in early 2010 that Americans' growing affluence over the past half-century has produced no measurable increase in overall happiness.

In fact, rates of depression are way up. Too many wealthy young Americans – whether celebrities or unknowns – are getting into more and more trouble with drugs, drunk driving, crime, gambling and divorce. And, in far too many instances, the family's affluence simply fuels that irresponsible, destructive behavior.

Paris Hilton may be the "poor little rich girl" poster child. The granddaughter of hotelier William Baron Hilton vaulted to celebrity status in 2003 after an x-rated video involving her was leaked to the Internet. In 2007, she was jailed for breaking a probation agreement relating to a drunk-driving charge. Nevertheless, she managed to leverage that infamy into $8 million worth of fashion contracts, appearance fees and television pay – in one year.

We may not be acquainted with the likes of Ms. Hilton, but we've all seen excessive consumption – and the trouble it can cause.

Make no mistake: Instilling disciplined financial attitudes in children is extremely challenging in a culture where the opportunities to succumb to Madison Avenue hype and easy credit are everywhere, and where the deplorable behavior of wealthy young celebrities is routinely glorified.

But putting most of the blame on outside influences may let parents off the hook too easily. So many wealthy parents are drawn into the trap of giving expensive *things* to their children that they destroy the children's motivation to find their own way, to develop their own potential, to create something of value, and to serve others.

"It's hard for wealthy parents to say 'no' because they don't have to," Buffone writes.

These problems are compounded when wealth passes in large chunks – think tens of trillions over the next four decades – to younger generations ill-equipped to manage it.

The Golden Handcuffs

Affluent families face many of the same challenges that the middle class does: Typically, both parents work outside the home, families eat together less often, divorce and frequent moves are common, extended families live farther away, technology and the media dominate daily life, children are overscheduled and overprotected, communities and churches have lost influence, schools are failing, and job opportunities have dwindled.

Add significant wealth, and these problems are magnified. Swaddled in the safety net their parents provide, many children of affluence feel no urgency to take charge of life. In the mistaken belief that "giving kids everything" will earn their love and respect, parents bankroll their children well into adulthood – unwilling to recognize that their "help" is thwarting their children's self-sufficiency.

Over several years of interviews with wealthy families, author and wealth counselor John L. Levy found that children of affluence typically experience delayed maturity; lack of motivation, self-discipline and accomplishment; guilt; boredom; an inability to relate to people of modest means; a paralyzing array of options; an inability to cope with others' resentment; and fear of losing wealth and having to support themselves.

> *"We have smaller families, we have more time to obsess about perfecting each child. Many parents can't stand to see their children unhappy or angry or disappointed ... . Our generation of parents is not happy themselves. A lot of women feel that their best emotional bet is their children."*
>
> – Madeline Levine, psychologist and author,
> The Price of Privilege

There's more. Other observers cite pressures to perform or to appear perfect, which become more evident as families get smaller. Affluenza also can breed neglect and estrangement.

Inside wealthy families, a number of factors can hamper the development of well-adjusted children. Parents can focus too much or too little on their children – neglecting them, coddling them or pressuring them to excel at all costs. Parents with high-powered careers often achieve their ascendancy by working long hours and traveling for the organization, cutting into the time they might spend with their children. Divorce and frequent relocations can deprive their children of the continuity, time-honored values and unconditional love that extended family can provide.

Parents who are successful at work often take a "businesslike" approach to childrearing: If efficiency can be achieved by having a maid make the children's beds, why take the time to insist that children do it themselves?

Fearful of allowing their children to taste the struggle that builds character, wealthy parents inadvertently prevent their children from learning economic self-sufficiency and resilience. What else would explain the high number of late-model cars seen in the student lots at suburban high schools – in the midst of a recession?

Eager to keep up appearances, affluent families have difficulty getting off the treadmill of high expectations – regarding what they can *buy* or *do,* as well as what they expect their children to *be.*

> *"High-achieving parents often apply the same business skills and acumen at home while raising their children, and they fail to realize that a different set of attitudes and behaviors is necessary to ensure that their children develop into adults with productive and fulfilling lives."*
>
> – Lee Hausner, psychologist and author,
> Children of Paradise

The luxuries that used to characterize an exceptional lifestyle have become the norm, and easy access to credit supports ever-more-conspicuous consumption.

Today, many American homes feature private, well-outfitted bedrooms and baths *for each child.* Such isolation exacerbates the bubble mentality, where the wealthy can barricade themselves in luxury while everyone else is forced to scramble for the remaining space.

Because they can afford it, affluent families are more likely to choose manufactured fun than the simple pleasures of walking, flying a kite or cooking a meal together.

Where families were once content to spend vacations camping, swimming, fishing, hiking or visiting relatives, they're now more likely to go to a theme park or multistar resort where every moment is scheduled, and little is left to chance or discovery. Prepackaged "vacation experiences" frequently deny families all-important opportunities to get to know one another better, in settings away from the busyness of day-to-day life.

Yet all those pleasures and luxuries have not created happier people.

Washington Post writer Sandra G. Boodman cites research showing that "affluent teens are among those least likely to receive treatment for emotional problems," because many of their parents are loath to mar the public image of the perfect family. One recent study found that upper-middle-class girls appear three times more likely to suffer from clinical depression.

> *"What affluent parents tend to do is see the child they wish they had – not the child they have. ... Parental love has become contingent on performance, which is very damaging."*
> – Madeline Levine, The Price of Privilege

High-profile parents face ever-greater pressures to maintain a façade of perfection, often denying their children the kind of adversity that helped strengthen their own character.

"Dynastic families raise their children under considerable pressure for high achievement and general excellence, (regardless of the children's talents or aptitudes)," writes wealth counselor Gerald Le Van. "It's also hard to establish an individual identity, rather than being seen as part of the family dynasty, particularly if the parents are well-known."

Le Van goes on to say that wealthy people often neglect their children. "They are busy and active. They can afford servants and boarding schools. But these are only second-class surrogates; they can't provide the personal attention and caring that children want from their parents."

Cut Off From Real Life

Children of wealth often feel disconnected from society, unable to relate to those of modest means. Guilty about living an easy life, they may struggle to cope with others' resentment. Many have trouble forming strong relationships.

Gated communities and exclusive clubs are, by nature, isolating. But for a child seeking peer acceptance, being labeled different can mean loneliness and ridicule. Potential playmates may be intimidated by a family's perceived wealth. Or a child may flaunt his status, driving away would-be friends.

"(Affluent people) may deny or avoid their power," Le Van continues. "They may misuse it arbitrarily, running roughshod over other people – overcompensating for a sense of inadequacy and confusion."

> *"If born to affluence, it's hard to understand the lives and experiences of persons in ordinary financial circumstances. Many inheritors feel uncomfortable with the power of their wealth, since they haven't earned it and don't deserve it."*
>
> – Gerald Le Van, wealth counselor
> and author, Raising Rich Kids

Children of wealth are so accustomed to their free ride that they may not even realize how entitlement and obsessive pleasure-seeking have crippled them. Many inheritors lack motivation, self-discipline and a sense of accomplishment. Some are so paralyzed by the diversity of their options that they fail to act at all. For many, the only well-paying job they can get is with the family business – where their underperformance can hamper the success of such enterprises.

Vast numbers of young Americans are learning at early ages that material wealth has little to do with hard work, achievement or patience. Instead, riches are theirs simply for having been born into a certain family.

Children who grow up eager to cash in on this birthright rarely develop the patience, work ethic or passion to achieve their own peak potential. Nor do youngsters accustomed to handouts develop an appreciation for what their parents or grandparents have provided.

Inheritors frequently have trouble launching a career. Because they don't need money from part-time jobs, they often fail to learn the employment or budgeting skills that their less-wealthy counterparts begin mastering as teens.

> *"The human mind, body and spirit thrive on struggle and challenge, just as a muscle thrives on exercise. Satisfaction without effort ... creates only dissipation, alienation, boredom, weakness and a sense of worthlessness."*
>
> – Dan Baker, What Happy People Know

Because they are not driven by life's necessities, Le Van says, inheritors' motivation can be brief and lacking intensity. They're easily frustrated and quick to give up when an obstacle presents itself. Some fear losing their family's money and being unable to make it on their own.

Children of affluence may have so many career options that they struggle to make decisions and set goals. Wealthy children rarely work their way through college and, because paying for it requires nothing of them, they appreciate it less.

> *"... Some wealthy children are underworked, not held to responsibilities and obligations, and therefore suffering from a certain crisis of utility, or agency – they've never had to do anything for themselves. These young people obsess, 'What can I do if I were left to my own resources entirely? How much of my success is really attributable to all the forms of help I get, and how much is really me?'"*
>
> – Suniya Luthar, psychologist, Columbia Teachers College

With so many wealthy, well-connected people disinclined or ill-equipped to manage the complex problems of the 21st century, what's to become of our society? Who will lead us? And will the old-fashioned values of honesty, industry, thrift, compassion, innovation and loyalty continue to fade?

As a report published by BMO Financial Group puts it:

> *"If an unwarranted ice cream cone or toy can send the wrong message to a middle-class child, imagine the impact on a child when a birthday party with celebrity guests, a new luxury car or a trip to Europe becomes a routine expectation. Such children tend to develop unreal expectations about life and family relationships, which may never be satisfied."*

Part II

Chapter 3
Building Resistance to Affluenza

I s it too late? Has affluenza already claimed our potential leaders – and the values that served previous generations so admirably?

In an attempt to answer the questions posed in Part I of this book, we undertook a series of interviews with individuals and families who seem to be defying the odds. Despite living amid an affluenza epidemic, they're demonstrating traditional values.

We looked for families with household assets equaling $3 million or more, excluding primary residences; a stake in a family business; and children age 20 or older who:

▓ Enjoy generally positive, long-term relationships with spouse, siblings, parents and others.

▓ Show evidence of hard work, focus and passion, regardless of whether the chosen occupation is lucrative.

▓ Select friends and partners based on traits such as honesty, loyalty and generosity.

▓ Are financially self-sustaining and live within their means.

▓ Contribute time, talent or money to groups such as youth sports clubs, neighborhood or civic groups, and church or temple.

We found that, despite media coverage that suggests most children of wealth are apathetic and self-absorbed, some affluent families *are* succeeding in raising grounded children.

In a culture in which many insecure parents constantly scurry to tend to their children's every desire, the parents we interviewed appeared focused on preparing their offspring to be self-sufficient, contributing adults.

We also spoke with one parent who admits he did many things poorly in raising a son overcome by affluenza – and offered his experience to serve as a cautionary tale.

While some readers may be horrified at the notion of shunning cable television or Christmas gifts, we found families who have the strength of will to do just that – untroubled by the endangered notion that discipline, accountability, tough lessons and delayed gratification are crucial in raising balanced children.

We talked with wealthy families who:

▪ Sit down to dinner together most evenings, and insist that everyone stays at the table until all are finished eating.

▪ Avoid the most prestigious school districts so their children will meet a greater diversity of students.

▪ Prefer camping in the rain to vacationing at luxury resorts.

▪ Resist the urge to purchase cable television and video games.

▪ Refuse to buy new cars for their children, and expect the children to pay for their own auto insurance.

▪ Expect their children to earn part of their college expenses.

▪ Send their teen on mission trips to developing countries.

▪ Adopt or foster-parent children from underprivileged backgrounds.

Deprivation? Hardly.

By looking at these families' philosophies and day-to-day behavior and decisions, we sought to learn more about what circumstances can help wealthy families create engaged offspring. We asked about meals, education, the family business, instilling a work ethic, philanthropy and volunteerism, having fun together, vacations, involvement of extended family, and religious observance.

While every family is unique – and no one can identify or control all of the factors that add up to success – we did find some common ground among our respondents. Specifically, the interviews showed that children of affluence tend to benefit from the following:

▪ Strong role models, often seen in relationships with grandparents. Frequent contact with extended family tends to reinforce the value systems of earlier generations, and some families go to great lengths to cultivate those relationships.

▓ Emphasis on philanthropy, volunteerism and job creation. In almost every case, respondent families demonstrate a strong commitment to the welfare of others.

▓ A willingness to let children find their own way, take responsibility for themselves and learn life's often-painful lessons.

▓ A commitment to getting to know one another in relaxed settings – by playing together, walking, working or just hanging out.

▓ A realistic notion of what hard work means.

▓ An expectation that educational systems and faith communities can do only so much, and that the buck stops with the family to provide solid grounding.

As well as these families have done, none is perfect. Many admit to questioning some aspects of their own upbringing, and they recognize their own mistakes – many of which were born of confusion, inexperience and societal pressures.

What these families do offer us is an antidote to the messages that our society delivers every day – messages that fuel Americans' addiction to consumption and an aversion to hard work and responsibility.

Without presenting themselves as heroes or experts, these families talk about their thought processes, their values and their practical ideas for raising well-rounded children. While most of what they say comes across as simple common sense, we've all seen how *un*common these attitudes can be among today's families – and the dispiriting results of that drift away from old-fashioned values.

Our interviewees provide practical examples of how they've held the line with their children. They describe how they have put a limit on luxuries, have insisted on chores at home, and have taught their children to take responsibility for their actions, desires and mistakes. They underline the importance of allowing their children to struggle and to endure disappointment – necessities on the path to discovering what life means and what's worth fighting for.

They talk about how they balance work and play. They emphasize how merely talking with and spending time getting to know their children, and letting their children know them, has strengthened bonds while allowing each child to develop his or her unique personality and purpose.

These parents also illustrate the value of constancy, of providing a steady, loving presence, and ensuring that their children connect meaningfully with extended family.

Our interviewees stress the importance of caring for others, through volunteer work, philanthropy or other community participation.

They also are gracious in sharing what they think they didn't do well.

While not everyone reading this will get another chance to raise children, younger readers may learn from our interviewees' mistakes and questions. By showing how possible it is to say "no" to a child when the entire culture seems to be screaming "go for it," these families offer support and insight to parents of wealth who grapple with similar concerns.

"Meals together send the message that citizenship in a family entails certain standards beyond individual whims. This is where a family builds its identity and culture. Legends are passed down, jokes rendered, eventually the wider world examined through the lens of a family's values. ... Younger kids pick up vocabulary and a sense of how conversation is structured. They hear how a problem is solved, learn to listen to other people's concerns and respect their tastes."

– Nancy Gibbs, writer,
The Magic of the Family Meal, TIME Magazine

Chapter 4
The Sacred Ritual of the Family Dinner

Family meals were a staple of my childhood, and my wife and I were determined to preserve the tradition as we raised our own children.

But in recent decades, I've observed more families allowing the family dinner to fade away. Parents are frequently working late or out of town, and children have sports practices or games. Fast food trumps home-cooked meals. Even when the family does sit down together, the television is often on and the children are texting their friends, diluting the value of this important ritual.

Our interviewees share my opinion on the need to preserve the family dinner.

> *"If it were just about food, we would squirt it into their mouths with a tube. A meal is about civilizing children. It's about teaching them to be a member of their culture."*
>
> – Robin Fox, anthropologist, Rutgers University

When Tina and George Schuman were raising their children, "family dinners were very important – the time at the end of the day when we would come together from five different directions," Tina says. "Eventually our kids had jobs, but we still tried to make it work."

George adds: "Everyone sat and we discussed things. Nobody left the table."

Faithful to his upbringing, Lou Schuman and his wife also make dinner with their young children a priority.

Similarly, Tom Abercrombie was raised to believe that "it's important to have dinner together and discuss the day. ... If I were going to be working late, I'd go home for dinner (and then back to work)."

"(That's the time when) I ask my kids about their days, and I tell them what we accomplished at work that day," says Tom, whose children range in age from 25 to 12. "I tell them I'm looking forward to tomorrow."

He strives to keep his own dinnertime conversation positive. "If I had a work problem to get off my chest, I wouldn't do it in front of the kids over dinner," Tom says.

Mealtime was cherished in the Robinson household as well. "Our parents were strict about dinner at 6," Ellen Robinson says. "And Sunday was family day; we couldn't be with friends on Sundays."

> *"The emotional and social benefits that come from family dinners are priceless. We know that teens who have frequent family dinners are likelier to get A's and B's in school and have excellent relationships with their parents. Having dinner as a family is one of the easiest ways to create routine opportunities for parental engagement and communication ... ."*
>
> – Elizabeth Planet, National Center on Addiction and Substance Abuse

After dinner, the sisters recall with fondness, "we'd walk together as a family, talking and sometimes going for ice cream." Both now insist that their small children sit down for family dinners.

Dave Smyth was home for dinner most nights. "The bell (at work) rang at 4:30, but I didn't want to fight traffic leaving downtown, so I waited until 6 to leave. Our family had dinner together. Afterward, my wife and

I did our own thing, while the kids went off to do their own thing."

When Larry Weathers was growing up, "we always had dinner together. My father came home at 6 for dinner to eat and watch the news. Outside of work, my father didn't do much except spend time with the family. He didn't drink or golf."

In his own household, however, the ritual is observed a little differently. "I'm home for dinner almost every night, but we don't eat as a family," Larry says. "The boys eat at 5 p.m. before I get home, though they'll sit with me while I eat. My wife is not a big eater and never sits down for dinner," though she spends time with the children at other times of the day.

Janine Harris recalls waiting for her father to come home so they could have dinner together, sometimes as late as 7:30 p.m.

"I was starving after school, but we had to wait," she says. "We always had Sunday dinner together, too, and were not allowed to go out with friends on Sundays."

Growing up in a household where mealtimes reigned supreme instilled in Janine the importance not only of preparing nutritious, delicious food but also sitting together and talking – however briefly – about the details of each person's day.

While most of the respondents view family mealtimes as a positive force, researchers point out that not every family obtains the same benefits. Meals can be rushed or argument-filled. In some houses, dinnertime conversation is thwarted by television watching and the use of cell phones and computers.

And those distractions, researchers say, can be a symptom of – or a contributor to – family distress.

"Compared to teens who have frequent family dinners without distractions at the table," a study by the National Center on Addiction and Substance Abuse has found, "those who have infrequent family dinners and say there are distractions at the table are three times likelier to use marijuana and tobacco, and two and a half times likelier to use alcohol."

And yet, the absence of cohesive dinner rituals does not necessarily mean children will grow up troubled.

Jeff Cosgrove recalls frequently missing dinner with his family because of the long hours he worked. And, like her father, Karen Cosgrove Sanders often was working or out of town while her husband and children were eating dinner together. When her children were preteens, however, Karen decided to take a few years off in order to spend more time with them.

During Harry O'Brian's youth, his family always ate together. And, for a while, so did his wife and children.

"We ate together most nights until about four years ago," says Harry, whose children are ages 20 to 11. "Now it's rare. We've fallen victim to busy schedules."

Harry's family is hardly alone. The addiction center's research suggests that about 40 percent of families do not eat dinner together five times a week.

Harry acknowledges that it's the job of the parents – not the children – to establish and enforce this practice. In his family, the lack of a united front undermined his efforts to preserve the family dinner.

"I wanted to keep pushing it," Harry says, "but my wife didn't insist on everyone eating together."

American society's diminished emphasis on the family dinner leaves one to wonder: If a family is not using mealtimes as a regular opportunity to communicate and impart values, just how will that family accomplish those important tasks?

> *"We've sold ourselves on the idea that teenagers are obviously sick of their families, that they're bonded to their peer group. We've taken it to mean that a teenager has no need for his family. And that's just not true. ...It's become a badge of honor to say, 'I have no time. I am so busy. But we make a lot of choices, and we have a lot more discretion than we give ourselves credit for."*
>
> – Miriam Weinstein, author,
> The Surprising Power of Family Meals

The Affluenza Antidote

"Studies have shown that when kids develop the capacity to work while in their teens, they stand a much better chance of discovering a satisfying career later in life. ... The capacity to work is one of the most significant developmental milestones in the transition to adulthood."

    – Gary Buffone, author, Choking on the Silver Spoon

Chapter 5
Instilling a Work Ethic and Respect for Money

As a teen, I could not have imagined not working. Because my father died while I was in high school, my family had little to spend on non-necessities, and I was eager for the cash flow, independence and social opportunities that a job would offer. Most of my friends worked summers during high school and part time in college while juggling studies and competitive sports. My children and their friends followed a similar routine.

> *"Work is important because it is a method of validating oneself (and) gives the individual the opportunity to experience the 'high' of achievement. When a child becomes addicted to the excitement of achievement, then money will not impair their productivity."*
>
> – Lee Hausner, psychologist and author,
> Children of Paradise

But what happens in wealthy families when young people do not work? Do those children develop job skills, an appreciation for money, and a sense of purpose in life – or do they fill their idle hours with pleasure-seeking and risk-taking behavior? Is it important for affluent families, who can afford to subsidize their children's leisure, to insist that their teenagers nevertheless take on some kind of employment?

Our interviews, along with the findings of various researchers, confirm my instincts and those of many others: That learning to work and to handle money are vital steps in a young person's development, and that parents in affluent families must make a special effort to promote work opportunities at virtually every stage of a child's growth.

Wise parents will stress that work is essential, not only for earning money and developing skills, but also for satisfying one's basic urge to feel engaged, fulfilled and successful. Could it be the very absence of meaningful work that drives many children of wealth to chase ill-advised thrill after thrill, futilely pursuing gratification in antisocial behavior?

For the Schuman family, instilling a work ethic and respect for money came naturally.

"George and I did what we learned growing up," Tina Schuman says. "We didn't hand our kids money. If they wanted something special, they had to earn it. If it was a big item, we might share the cost with them."

> *"Parents must give children the opportunity to want something badly enough to go after it themselves."*
>
> – Gary Buffone, Choking on the Silver Spoon

George Schuman recalls that their children started around age 5 performing simple household chores, like clearing the table. They then graduated to doing yard work for pay, earning 25 cents for each tree they mulched. By their mid-teens, they were all working after-school or summer jobs – in the factory or office of their father's business, mowing and weeding, or employed at local retail outlets and restaurants.

When they wanted extra cash for an eagerly awaited concert, he recalls, they each took on extra landscaping chores at home to earn the $30 ticket price.

When their sons began to drive, Tina says, they either accepted hand-me-down vehicles or saved enough money to afford a modest car – with a match from their parents. As a result of these disciplines, Tina says, "our kids had a good handle on what money did. They weren't entitled or overindulged."

Lou does recall catching a break once, however, when he put a golf ball through a window and his parents paid for the repair.

> *"Work that fulfills is critically important to inheritors' welfare. Few of us can maintain our self-esteem without working. ... Most inheritors like work situations where they are not perceived as 'different.'"*
>
> – Gerald Le Van, author, Raising Rich Kids

Larry Weathers' growing up was characterized by moderation and patience.

"My parents and grandparents were very conservative; there was very little over the top," he says. "We could have lived in a fancier neighborhood, but we led a very middle-class life."

"My sister and I didn't get a weekly allowance," Larry recalls. "My parents bought my clothes, but they didn't buy toys except for birthdays and Christmas. I had to wait for my things" – in one case waiting more than a year for a coveted item.

As a high-schooler, Larry says he "did grunt work (in the family business), filling propane tanks. I froze my tail off, but I was eager to earn my stripes."

Because modest living was all Larry knew, he says, he didn't wish for more luxuries. His parents, wanting to protect him from pressure to join the family enterprise, also didn't talk business at home.

"My parents did a nice job of raising me," Larry says, and he's passing along the lessons to the next generation. Recently, his young son found a game that was to be his gift for an upcoming birthday.

"He wanted to open it," Larry says, "but I'm making him wait. He's not happy but has accepted it. He didn't throw the game on the ground. I'll thank him for understanding that he needs to wait, that patience has its rewards."

Where Larry's family didn't talk business at home, the Cosgroves did just the opposite. Jeff and Ann's two daughters, Karen and Lisa, loved discussing real estate over dinner and helping their parents with ongoing remodeling projects at home.

The girls earned money by babysitting and helping in their father's office. As a family, they also enjoyed scouting furniture at antique stores – a love that has endured into adulthood. Karen and Lisa researched the pieces, and the Cosgroves sold them at auction – sometimes at a nifty profit. The proceeds bolstered the girls' college funds.

> *"Children can't learn to become emotionally resilient if they don't get regular practice handling failure and frustration. ... A little hardship is a necessary catalyst for success."*
>
> – Gary Buffone, Choking on the Silver Spoon

Among thoughtful parents, developing and enforcing allowance policies generates lively debate. Should children be paid for the services they perform around the house and yard? How formally should allowances be structured?

Karen Cosgrove Sanders recalls getting an allowance of $100 per quarter when growing up – and admits abusing it.

"(It) wasn't clearly defined who'd pay for what," she says. "I learned to game the system and spend my allowance early, and then my parents would bail me out and buy me things I needed."

Karen set up a detailed allowance system for her own two children that teaches money skills while acknowledging the privilege of being "part of a successful family." The system has taken the drama out of most purchasing decisions, she says, while giving the children responsibility for and control over their own budgets.

Originally, "my daughter and I had a lot of conflicts when shopping for clothes," Karen says. "She wanted trendy brand names when something else would do. If I were paying, I would insist on approving the purchase, and I would ask her to choose something less expensive. We debated constantly."

"When she was 12 or 13," Karen continues, "we created an allowance system that would give her $150 a month and allow her to make

The Affluenza Antidote

her own decisions regarding clothes, snacks, movies, music, games, gifts for her friends and donations to charity. My husband and I would continue paying for education, meals with family, special event clothes, underwear, sporting gear, and basic cell phone service – things we still controlled."

Both of the Sanders children – one in college and another about to start – track every purchase in an Excel spreadsheet that Karen set up, and spending is reviewed monthly.

"At the time, $150 felt like a lot," Karen says. With the system in place, though, both have "become much more frugal and have wanted to save quite a bit." Her son, in particular, doesn't like to spend money and is very generous to charitable organizations.

The children are still expected to help around the house.

> "Parents have to give their children opportunities to be competent as often as possible."
>
> – Lee Hausner, Children of Paradise

Karen notes that her system, like her parents', has flaws. "My daughter likes expensive clothes but won't pay for most of them, so we still negotiate because she loves the control."

"People have criticized me for being so money-focused," she admits, and also recognizes the controversy surrounding "doing business deals" with one's children. As well, Karen and her husband Tim understand why some parents might feel conflicted in pushing teens to land fast-food jobs just to earn money.

"Tim wants them to do educational things and help them learn and grow," she says. "He hasn't wanted them to do menial jobs." By providing allowances, Tim and Karen are freeing their children to pursue internships and volunteer work that develop meaningful skills but pay little or nothing.

"Our son is now finishing his third summer (in a low-paid but meaningful internship)," she says. "He's getting a great education and challenge." Their daughter has volunteered for two summers in an inner-city program.

In the end, Karen acknowledges that parents "can't *make* their kids do something; a lot is in genes. But you *can* show your kids by example how you make decisions about spending and how you treat other people. You can give them the right incentives and motivation, and turn responsibility over to them."

She advises parents: "If you decide on an allowance, stick with it."

Libraries, bookstores and the Internet provide resources for helping parents teach their children to value money.

Charles W. Collier, senior philanthropic adviser at Harvard University, offers some practical suggestions: "When children are in grade school, it's appropriate to ... structure an allowance, provide jobs for pay, encourage long-term savings (and) set limits around money. ... In the teen years, experts suggest that parents insist on summer employment (and guide children) through their budget."

Tom Abercrombie grew up with a strong sense of the connection between hard work and money.

> *"Unless at least one parent is working, their children will not see a model of work in their family and may not understand the value of working and being motivated to work themselves."*
>
> – Lee Hausner, Children of Paradise

"Both of my parents worked hard and created value for the dollar," he says. "I felt it was important to work. ... I was around some other kids who were spoiled by their parents, and I saw the difference between those who learned to work and those who didn't."

To help ensure that his own children would understand where money came from, "we told them when they were young that their mother and I worked hard, got lucky breaks and were able to buy extras, like a cottage and a ski chalet. We have those because we get up every day and go to work."

Tom adds: "We talk about money openly in our house. We tell the kids: 'Mom and I made (our money). You're entitled to some benefits, like living in the house with us, but you'll have to go out and make your own."'

The Abercrombie children bought in: By age 13 or 14, they were getting summer jobs.

Tom has discouraged his children from counting on inheritances to spare them from establishing their own careers. He's told them: "We'll die in our 90s, so you'll be your 60s or 70s when you get your inheritances. We're leaving most of our money to charity anyway, so it'll be easier to just get jobs."

He doesn't give his children an allowance – instead encouraging babysitting, mowing and odd jobs – but acknowledges that his "wife would sneak money to them behind my back." He also insisted that any outside help the family hires must not clean the children's rooms.

> *"Don't take away the opportunity for a child to make it on his or her own."*
>
> – Barton Goldsmith, psychotherapist and syndicated columnist

When Tom's children began thinking about cars, "we said we'd match every dollar they put in but they'd have to pay their own insurance. I took them to visit the insurance agent personally so they'd understand what was involved. As soon as they got their first ticket and the insurance premium went up, they became more responsible drivers."

"My son went into shock when his insurance doubled (because he'd gotten a ticket)," Tom says. "He had to take his car off the road for a while. The younger ones tried to hold off on driving so as not to get tickets."

Dave Smyth recalls his wife enforcing rules around chores and allowances when their children were young.

"My kids developed a work ethic (by helping around the house)," he says. "Their allowances weren't large, but they didn't goad me for more money. They seemed to appreciate the advantages they had."

These days, Dave admires the motivation that his grandchildren display. The family owns several cabins in the Poconos, and "it's typical of my grandchildren to want to come for the summer and work.

One wanted to drive the drink wagon around a golf course. Two of my grandchildren's friends also came to live here and work for the summer."

Had any of his children asked for an expensive car for his or her 16th birthday, claiming that "everybody" was getting one, Dave would have refused.

Ellen and Laura Robinson, on the other hand, had plenty of comforts handed to them as children – clothing, entertainment, cars and the occasional bailout.

"I had a car accident that was my fault," Laura says, "but my parents paid for the repairs and the increased insurance."

Still, they developed a strong work ethic, holding jobs as teenagers and today running successful businesses.

Similarly, Janine Harris was given a steady stream of luxuries – and nevertheless developed a taste for hard work.

"I knew nothing but private schools, the nicest stores, nicer sit-down restaurants, and shopping trips to New York City," she recalls. "Many of my friends were bluebloods who lived in big houses at the most prestigious addresses."

"As a kid, I worked in my Dad's businesses, though I never went and got a job," Janine says. Though she didn't need the money, "I got there at 6 a.m. and worked hard. My parents paid for my car and bought all my clothes and gas. I didn't really have any expenses (other than going) out with friends or buying gifts for my parents."

She recalls the comfort of knowing "my parents would provide for me no matter what," even into adulthood.

But Janine recognized the strings attached, including the pressure to keep up appearances as a wealthy family. As Janine matured, she says, "I felt I needed to change that." Eventually, she married a "very grounded, not wealthy" husband who "balanced me and helped me to see life as it really is."

Harry O'Brian, who worked hard as a youth, acknowledges the lost opportunities to develop a better work ethic and financial literacy in his own children.

"When I was growing up, my parents didn't have as much money as we do (now)," he says. "If I wanted a non-necessity like a camera or camping event, I'd have to pay for it, or my parents might chip in if they thought it was a good idea. Or I'd wait until my birthday, when they might offer to pay half. Nonessentials were a rare treat, not like the volume of stuff my kids want and get now."

Harry continues: "As a kid, I always had a few hundred dollars, which was enough money to do what I needed. At age 12, I began babysitting, and my brothers got jobs to save up for bikes and other wants."

His parents became significantly wealthier when just one sibling was still at home. "The three oldest in our family 'softened up the target' for the youngest, who got more stuff because our parents had much more money. My older siblings and I joked that 'if Peter was grounded, he couldn't take the corporate jet.'"

Harry's youngest brother "worked as little as possible," he recalls. Harry suspects that Peter subscribed to a different mentality, believing that he "might be set with the family's money" and would never have to earn his own way.

> *"Kids should have chores. A lot of kids I see don't have to do anything except shine. (That's how parents) turn out narcissistic or self-centered kids. As one girl I see told me, 'If I'm so special, why do I have to clear the table?'"*
>
> – Madeline Levine, author, The Price of Privilege

In contrast to Harry's experience as a youth, "my own son didn't get his first job until age 20. There was no good reason for him not to have a job in high school. Our 17-year-old has only babysat because she's busy with soccer and needs to concentrate on school."

Harry also admits that "my wife and I have been inconsistent with our kids' allowances. At times they had allowances for doing chores, but the rules were not always clear. If one wanted an iPod or something worthwhile, we would match funds. Otherwise, they'd pay all of it. But they didn't have to wait or work hard to earn the money, because they get 'laundered money from Grandma' and other relatives. They always had $100 or $200 that they didn't work for."

Harry adds: "My kids don't do a lot around the house. Taking the garbage out requires five reminders. My wife does the lion's share of cleaning, and I help with dishes. I do the yard work and outside maintenance. Only occasionally do the kids clean their own bedrooms; we gave up pushing them to do it."

He reflects: "I've talked a lot about the value of money, but we didn't have enough discipline. My wife and I were not always on the same page, and so were paralyzed. If I could do it over again, I'd start early to establish a structure around allowances and household chores, whether my wife agreed or not. I would probably mandate getting a part-time job at a certain age."

Harry and his wife have purchased used cars for the two oldest and are paying for insurance and major repairs. The children have to pay for gas, oil, accessories and any traffic tickets.

He expects his children will experience an abrupt awakening at some point. "My kids want to make a lot of money so they can live the same lifestyle they enjoy now," he says, but "they don't understand what's involved," or how hard they'll have to work to earn that much.

"(But my kids) know that they have to have careers," Harry says. "None of them expects we'll give them fun money."

Still, age and experience have given them some perspective. Economic diversity is evident among their public-school classmates.

"When our kids were littler, they asked, 'Daddy, why don't we have a bigger house?' As teens, they say: 'Why do my friends think we live in a mansion? I'm embarrassed because my friend thinks we're rich. Are we rich?' I tell them that we're doing better than most."

Harry stops short of criticizing modern parenting. "We all read that baby boomers coddle kids, and kids expect more. But I don't think things are going to hell in a hand basket. Today's kids are more creative. Some traditional disciplines seem silly to me, like making kids pay for everything."

Dan Wilson was born before World War II, and he reflects on how that era shaped him.

"My father made $12 a week," he recalls. "We didn't have a car or TV until I was a preteen. Most of our budget went toward food and shelter. We didn't go to fancy restaurants or take vacations. I started

The Affluenza Antidote

working at age 12. My father made me earn the money for a bike, and I had to buy my own car."

However, "by the time my younger sisters came along, my parents were doing better, and so the girls lived a more prosperous life, including regular vacations."

Dan started his business four decades ago, when his children were very young and he wasn't wealthy. "They've seen the family business develop from scratch."

His son demonstrated diligence when he came to work for his father while in high school. But once he obtained stock and unearned income from the business, he seemed to lose the desire to work, Dan laments.

"My lawyer had suggested I gift the maximum amount every year to my kids since they were born," to get it out of his estate, Dan says. But he didn't realize the negative impact this would have, making life so easy for his son that he's never established himself in a career, or even held a regular job for an extended period.

Looking back, Dan is now clear: "It's a bad idea to allow large inheritances from one generation to another. I gave my kids too much too soon."

Goldsmith, the psychotherapist, would agree:

> *"It is important that parents don't give their children so much that they aren't motivated to do things for themselves."*

"The amount of playtime kids have has shrunk by 25 percent in the last 20 years."

– Richard Louv, author, Last Child in the Woods

Chapter 6
Cherishing Old-Fashioned Fun

Having fun has gotten very expensive.

When our family was young, evening entertainment consisted of several families gathering for a dinner we prepared together in one of our homes. Once infants were bedded in portable cribs for the evening, we adults engaged in conversation or played cards or board games.

These days, in most affluent households, it seems it's hard to have fun without an Internet connection and an electronic application for everything from cooking to chess.

Has old-fashioned fun – like skipping stones, flying kites or playing board games – become too quaint a notion for today's upscale families? Consider this: A Google search for "Nintendo" will turn up 122 million pages, while a search for "backgammon" scores a mere 8 million.

How important is it for families who can easily afford all the latest electronics to turn off Wii in favor of a walk in the woods? Do children of affluence grow up thinking that fun always requires spending money? Must organized sports be pursued so relentlessly that children have no free time to exercise their imaginations? Does the glut of Internet and cable TV options discourage outdoor play – eroding opportunities for families and neighbors to get to know one another?

Some researchers say that too much time in front of a screen and too little time in nature contribute to childhood depression, obesity and attention-deficit disorder.

Make no mistake. Americans are simply not as close to nature as we used to be. Nicholas Kristof writes in *The New York Times*: "Only 2 percent of American households now live on farms, compared with 40 percent in 1900. Suburban childhood that once meant catching snakes in fields now means sanitized video play dates scheduled a week in advance."

Kristof adds: "One study of three generations of 9-year-olds found that by 1990 the radius from the house in which they were allowed to roam freely was only one-ninth as great as it had been in 1970."

How are affluent families particularly affected? They may live in gated or covenanted communities where play equipment and even vegetable gardens are controlled or prohibited, and where surveillance systems discourage roaming.

Today's parents are more fearful than ever of accidents, molestations and abductions. Photos of missing children are printed on milk cartons, and the movements of sex offenders are publicized. Stories of children kidnapped and murdered are a staple of news programs and talk shows.

> *"So where is the greatest danger? Outdoors, in the woods and fields? Or on the couch in front of the TV? A blanket wrapped too tightly has its own consequences. One is that we may end up teaching our children ... that life is too risky but also not real ... ."*
>
> – Richard Louv, Last Child in the Woods

Increasingly, concerns over liability are driving communities and school districts to dumb down playground equipment, outlaw skateboarding and otherwise limit free play.

For children of wealth, easy access to every new electronic toy ensures that they'll be continuously entertained – indoors.

As children spend less unstructured time with peers, they also miss out on vital life lessons like taking turns and coping with "unfairness." On the playground, children once learned to fall and to pick themselves up. In the woods, they discovered the wonders – and the unhurried pace – of the natural world. Today, many children do neither.

Fortunately, some affluent families still insist that their children pursue unstructured play time, preferably outside. They recognize that unscripted time can present precious opportunities for making friends and bonding with family members.

Tom Abercrombie recalls that his children didn't watch much television while growing up. After school, they would do homework, play a game or, when they were older, go to a sports practice. Among them, his children pursued soccer, hockey, baseball and sailing.

"We usually put them in one organized sport so they could learn teamwork," he recalls. "We didn't drive them around all day long."

Instead, other children visited the Abercrombie home. "Our house was the gathering house," he says, "and we kept an eye on the kids."

Tom and his wife have resisted the trend that has more and more children glued to a screen for hours each day.

"I see (video games) as mindless entertainment," Tom says. "Though every other kid had an Atari game, we never bought it for our kids, and we wouldn't allow them to use their money to buy it."

Only recently did the Abercrombies buy a television for their ski chalet, and they don't subscribe to cable – demonstrating to their children how limited television was a generation ago. Because the channels are few and the reception poor, "the kids get bored with TV. They would rather play in the snow."

Tom and his wife have preferred to emphasize games and toys "that stretch kids' imagination and knowledge." When his children were younger, they would play with Legos and train sets for hours, he says.

For Larry Weathers, video games are best used as a tool for sharing leisure time with his children. But he'd rather see the children playing outside.

"We live in a safe, quiet neighborhood with lots of kids," Larry says. "My kids swim, play pickup ball games, bicycle and play on the swing set. They're learning to play golf."

Still, he acknowledges that times have changed. "When I was growing up, my siblings and I ran around outside," he recalls. "We lived on a main street, and my grandparents lived behind us, on a side street with kids of all ages. We spent 90 percent of our time there."

When young Larry expressed interest in a video game, his parents balked. "I waited for more than a year for a Nintendo game console. I didn't get it until the second Christmas I asked for it."

Like many parents, Lou Schuman would like his children to play outside as much as he did when young. "We have to drag our kids outside," he says. "Our 5-year-old would rather read a book."

When they do venture outdoors, Lou and his children ride bikes, kick balls, or play in the sandbox or on the swing set. They particularly enjoy physical touch, including wrestling and horseplay.

The experts reinforce the value of that kind of togetherness. Buffone writes: "Children need attention, affection, time, guidance, space and safe places where they can learn and feel secure. They need play, touching, jokes, conversation and unconditional caring."

"As a kid," Lou says, "we had a one-hour limit on TV watching, which our Mom enforced. We had to fill out a sheet on the refrigerator. We had a few computer games, but those also were subject to time limits."

"I complained at the time," Lou says, but he has followed his parents' practice of limiting his children's time with electronics.

Tina Schuman's memory meshes with her son's. "I did limit their television time to maybe 30 to 60 minutes after homework was done. They also watched Saturday morning cartoons. Sometimes the whole family watched TV programs together."

But the bigger draw was the large piece of property that the family lived on, with a pool, tennis courts and woods in which the boys rode motorized bikes. "As a kid, I lived in the woods," Lou says.

George Schuman recalls: "The boys played pickup basketball games with friends, climbed trees and rode go-karts. In winter, they would sled or ride their grandfather's snowmobile."

In so many ways, wealthy parents can make outdoor recreation particularly attractive, with pools and tennis courts at home, and mountain or waterfront property for weekend boating, hiking or skiing.

Dan Wilson and his wife and children enjoyed playing doubles on their home tennis court. He also remembers his children riding bikes and playing outside regularly. They walked to and from events at school a half-mile away. The family bought a computer when one child was 14, but Dan doesn't recall either child spending excessive time in front of a TV or computer screen.

Dave Smyth says his children played outside often. Other than Scout camps and music lessons, he doesn't recall them having lots of structured activities.

> *"We get on (our children's) backs when they sit in front of the TV, and then we tell them to go outside and play. But where? How? Join another organized sport? Some kids don't want to be organized all the time. They want to let their imaginations run; they want to see where a stream of water takes them."*
>
> – Richard Louv, Last Child in the Woods

Why has organized play become controversial? Many say that too much structure crowds out free play, and that excessive organization or adult interference raises children's anxiety and hampers their development and creativity.

Even worse is the tendency of some parents to overreact at children's games – some even arguing with coaches and referees or screaming at their children for botching a play.

The Robinson sisters encourage their young children to play outdoors often. In bad weather, Ellen says, "I encourage them to play basketball and tennis in the basement."

Ellen and Laura recall that, as children, "if it was nice out, we were kicked out. We never fought our parents about going outside."

They didn't watch much television or play computer games. "There wasn't much on TV at that time anyway," Laura recalls.

Ellen says her children are too young right now for electronics but wonders about the benefits. "I hear that video games are good for improving dexterity," she says, though she also knows of studies that discourage exposing children to electronics.

Laura believes that educational videos – those that teach math, art or music – can be valuable if chosen carefully and not overused.

Tim and Karen Sanders say that electronics were indeed beneficial when their son was small and too active to sit and watch TV. "The early kids' computer games were helpful because they got him to focus," Karen says.

The Sanders children played outside often – not so much with neighbors, though, because their house was too far out. Even today – with their children nearly grown – the family enjoys playing board games and spending weekends at their lake house.

While some parents are attempting to raise their own children much as their parents raised them, Harry O'Brian notes an "amazing difference" between how his children spend their free time and how he did.

Back then, he says, "we had four channels; cable was too expensive. We watched five or six favorite shows, plus sports. Our mother often pushed us to turn off TV and go outside (where) hundreds of kids" lived in his neighborhood. "We had a lot of neighborhood pickup games and even organized our own leagues."

He and his brothers rode bikes and competed with one another and their father in basketball. "My Dad spent a lot of time with us and came to our games. Mom drove us to everything."

When his own children were younger, he recalls, they sometimes played outside, though their neighborhood didn't have as many other children living nearby.

"I'd take them to the park or playground, and I'd teach my son to play baseball," Harry recalls. "We picked berries together. Or they'd have a friend over and we'd all swim in the pool." The family often watched television together or went shopping.

"Before we had computers," Harry says, "they played outside more. Now they have zero interest in going outside to play, and we rarely tell them to. ... My son spends a lot of time on the computer, and our older daughter likes texting."

"They're the MTV generation," he acknowledges. "We have a million channels, and there's a greater variety on TV."

In addition, Harry laments that, as his children moved into their teen years, "our together time dropped off. My son's in college and our older daughter is rarely home. Our little one and I are most likely to hang out."

The researchers, though, would applaud Harry's willingness to spend time together, without an agenda. Wealth counselor and author Gerald Le Van writes that "parents need to be there for what may come up when nothing seems to be happening."

To paraphrase a popular television commercial (yes, even Madison Avenue gets it right occasionally!):

Dollars spent = zero.
Hanging out with one's child = priceless.

"All the expensive toys, cars and exotic vacations in the world can't replace a child's feeling of being loved ... . Making them feel loved requires our time and energy, not our cash."

– Gary Buffone, author, Choking on the Silver Spoon

Chapter 7
Vacations and Extended Family

In decades past, American children typically lived among extended family and in ethnically cohesive neighborhoods – circumstances that helped define identity and provide a blanket of love and security. With family members living close by, children usually had several important kin with whom to share the good times and from whom to seek support during the difficult ones.

> *"What children need most are the essentials that grandparents provide in abundance. They give unconditional love, kindness, patience, humor, comfort, lessons in life – and, most importantly, cookies."*
>
> – Rudolph Giuliani, former mayor, New York City

Today, such closeness is harder to come by. As advances in technology and transportation, along with career pressures and opportunities, increasingly spread affluent families around the country and the globe, many children lack the bonding opportunities that would help them develop a healthy identity. For such families, cultivating that security and long-term view requires special effort.

In my own family, togetherness has been a priority throughout childhood and adulthood. And, as our extended family has grown, we have found ourselves fortunate to enjoy the resources to visit one another often and to vacation together.

If our interviews are any indication, it turns out that quality time with extended family – particularly grandparents – indeed may be vital to raising well-adjusted, generous children. As in my own family, our interviewees say that vacationing with grandparents and other relatives presents an ideal opportunity to bond – regardless of how posh the locale.

In the experts' eyes as well, creating memories and sharing adventures with grandparents, aunts, uncles and cousins are far more important to raising motivated children than being pampered in five-star resorts, which raises too-high expectations about how leisure time will be spent.

When Dave Smyth's children were small, the family and some friends spent a couple of weeks each summer at a lodge in the Poconos. Later, the Smyths and two other families bought an old inn and several cabins on the shore of a lake.

"The cabins were rustic, slightly better than camping," Dave says, and "we had our meals in the lodge."

Days were spent outdoors – boating, fishing, hiking, golfing, swimming. Decades later, Dave still spends summers at the camp. His children and grandchildren visit every year, some coming from thousands of miles away.

"I like having young people around. I encourage my grandchildren to bring their friends," Dave says. "It's a wonderful place."

Some of his grandchildren and their friends have worked resort jobs and stayed all summer – sleeping in rooms affectionately dubbed the "dormitory."

"We're generating memorable experiences for the next generation," Dave says.

At least once a year, the Robinson sisters take their children on vacation with grandparents. When they travel with their father, they often ski and enjoy "good conversations on the chairlifts." With their mother, they're more likely to take a warm-weather trip to swim or golf.

Dan Wilson and his wife also oriented many vacations around grandparents, either on Martha's Vineyard or in Florida.

The Cosgrove family owned land with cabins in the Adirondacks, where they camped often. When Jeff's work took him to England, Ann and the girls went along to stay with Ann's family in Europe.

Early exposure to international travel may have stimulated Karen Cosgrove Sanders' appetite for faraway places – eventually leading her and Tim to buy property in the Canadian Rockies where they and their children ski, hike, fish and swim.

Like most of those interviewed, "vacations were a priority for my parents," Lou Schuman says. "We usually stayed in modest places, motels that had a pool or beach. For ski trips, we'd usually stay above a bar."

They went camping, sometimes with other families, and drove to Daytona Beach every spring break for 15 years, say George and Tina Schuman.

With their children, Lou and his wife often visit friends from past jobs or graduate school. "We do a lot of camping and hiking," Lou says. "Our kids love the adventure of sleeping in a tent."

He and his wife also appreciate the opportunity to "have a lot of good conversations" with other parents and see how they manage challenging situations.

"Once, we went camping with another family in the rain," he said. "It was more a community thing and less about comfort or eating at a fancy restaurant. We had a great time."

The experience epitomizes one of Lou's parenting goals: "I aspire to quality time and memories, rather than having a big boat, car or house."

Common to our interviewees is the premium placed on time spent with extended family. Most would agree that the grandparent-grandchild relationship is a special one that's worth nurturing.

"Grandparents on both sides are in town, and most of our cousins also live here, so we see extended family a lot," Karen Sanders says. "We frequently host big family get-togethers at our lake house."

Her parents made sure that Karen and her sister saw their relatives regularly.

"We spent a lot of time with my wife's parents, who had a farm nearby," Jeff Cosgrove says, "and we saw my mother frequently, as well as my brother's children. My daughter Lisa is particularly close to one cousin."

While geographic proximity makes it easier to stay in touch, connectedness needn't suffer when branches of a family are separated by thousands of miles. The Cosgroves crossed the Atlantic more than once to cultivate their daughters' relationships with family members abroad.

On the other hand, living nearby doesn't guarantee emotional closeness.

Lou Schuman "didn't really connect" with his cousins who lived in a nearby city. Though they celebrated most holidays and some birthdays together, age differences presented obstacles.

As for cousins in his own city, "there are several I'd like to be closer with." He notes that, over the last decade, his mother has "made new connections" with family living in the area.

Lou's own children spend more time with cousins than he did – going camping with his brother's family, for example – but there's "still room for improvement."

Lou admires his wife's family, which maintains close connections despite living hundreds of miles apart. "We go there every holiday. Her family is a better model. Everyone lives close to one another, and it's easy to show up and hang out."

Whether extended family lives on the same street or a continent away, advocates say, close relationships with grandparents and other relatives can be invaluable in helping raise a healthy, well-adjusted child.

> *"(Grandparents) are good teachers, having practiced on their children."*
>
> – Kathryn M. McCarthy, director of client services,
> Rockefeller & Company

Lou and his siblings were tight with grandparents on both sides, George Schuman recalls. Tina's father, who lived in the same city, was "the neatest grandfather anyone could have." He had a fascinating job as a sports agent and was involved in boxing as well. His life "revolved around our kids," George says, letting them ride his snowmobile and getting them freebies through his work and volunteer connections.

George's own father, who lived 100 miles away and spent time in Florida, was more reserved and formal, and provided a "good contrast" to their flamboyant maternal grandfather. When one of George's sons was only 6, he traveled by plane to visit George's parents in Florida. "When the kids stayed with (my parents), they always had a great time."

Larry Weathers grew up a short walk away from his grandparents' house – an arrangement that he considered idyllic.

"Kids of all ages lived in their neighborhood," he recalls, "and we spent 90 percent of our time there."

Several aunts and uncles lived nearby as well, and "we had dinner together with the extended family a lot. We'd have big family gatherings at our grandparents' house, especially during summer."

> *"Excessive ... trips load too much pressure and activity on kids who would do better just playing in the yard."*
>
> – BMO Financial Group,
> Raising Healthy Children in Families of Affluence

When Larry was in eighth or ninth grade, his parents bought a timeshare condominium in Florida that his mother still owns.

"My wife loves it," he says. "We take our kids there, and sometimes my wife's sister. It's very mellow. We enjoy just sitting in the water."

In the Robinson family, both sets of grandparents lived nearby. One summer the girls lived with their paternal grandparents while their mother and father traveled.

As a child, Harry O'Brian enjoyed his immediate family's summer ritual of renting a cottage in New England. But he was keenly aware of living far from extended family, whom he saw only at Thanksgiving.

Harry has been determined to make things different for his own children. Their vacations typically involve visiting his parents or in-laws in Florida or Cape Cod, where they go boating, play tennis, take walks or lie on the beach.

But he and his siblings are not content to limit their together time to an annual vacation. "We have made it a point to live near one another and have frequent contact," Harry says.

While his wife's family lives out of state, "my kids have very extensive connections on my side," Harry says. "For the last 11 years, we've lived within a mile of my parents."

Harry's children see them often, sometimes daily, and "my parents have been able to come to the kids' plays and sporting events."

Some who study social patterns suggest that extended-family living may be enjoying a resurgence.

"We've gone through a 50- to 60-year experiment with nuclear families, and now we're headed back toward more extended-family living," says John L. Graham, marketing professor at the University of California/Irvine. "It's in our nature as human beings to live together."

The benefits that all enjoy when extended family members develop strong relationships are immeasurable. Particularly when children are at odds with their own parents, grandparents can provide precious attention, affection, stability and guidance.

> *"Affluent children can be given so much that they focus on their own needs to the exclusion of others. (Children exposed to philanthropy see that) satisfaction can be derived from money not just because it enables them to buy whatever they want, but because it can create better lives for others. ... (Philanthropy) gives them a profound sense of their place in the world."*
>
> – Eileen and Jon Gallo, authors, Silver Spoon Kids: How Successful Parents Raise Responsible Children

Among our interviewees, the geographic proximity of at least one set of grandparents appears to be a difference maker. In most, the engagement in a family business – typically started by grandparents or with grandparents' money – can provide role modeling of values and an expression of the family's identity in the community. Such intimate interaction with grandparents – products of the 1930s Depression – assures the grandchildren exposure to the core values of what Tom Brokaw has called the Greatest Generation.

For modern families challenged by geographic distance, technology also can help. Easily accessible innovations like Skype allow grandchildren and grandparents to see one another as they talk, getting to know each other better and reinforcing those intergenerational connections. In my family, communicating frequently via Skype allows us to connect even more meaningfully when we do vacation together.

Social scientists agree that children who develop a strong sense of their identity and family's history typically end up far more centered than those disconnected from past generations. My own experience and observations bear this out.

On this point, the anthropologist Margaret Mead was unequivocal:

"In order to be a full human being ...
everyone needs to have access
both to grandparents and grandchildren."

"(Parents) are going to transfer legacies of meaning as well as financial wealth, whether they think about it or not."

– Paul Schervish, director,
Social Research Institute, Boston College

Chapter 8
Modeling Philanthropy and Volunteerism

When I refer to the wealthy families I have gotten to know over my three-decade career, so far I have emphasized the negative.

But, to be fair, I also must underline what those people as a group have tended to do extremely well: give back to society. I have been impressed and humbled many times over by the commitment of my clients – and many other wealthy folks I have met through board memberships – to improve their own communities and beyond.

Certainly, tax considerations have encouraged some of their largesse. But in most of my clients, I have seen a heartfelt desire to share, to empower, to provide a hand up to those who struggle with undeserved burdens.

> *"If you're going to raise responsible children in an affluent environment, philanthropy – the desire to help mankind – must be part of your value system."*
>
> – Gallo and Gallo, Silver Spoon Kids

In fact, talking with my clients about the causes that attracted not just their money but also their time and attention was perhaps the most gratifying aspect of my work. For many patriarchs and matriarchs, seeing their children and grandchildren poised to carry on their philanthropic legacy often fulfills perhaps their deepest wish.

I was not surprised, then, to see philanthropy and volunteerism emerge as important among our interviewees – as opportunities for addressing societal needs as well as raising children with a balanced perspective on life.

Social observers agree.

"(Research shows a) striking correlation between a feeling of social responsibility, and comfort and satisfaction with being affluent," writes wealth counselor Gerald Le Van. "Giving or investing for the benefit of society can provide a sense of meaning and purpose."

Imagine a Christmas morning in the home of a very affluent family – and no gifts under the tree.

Tom Abercrombie describes how this scenario came to occur in his household: "A local charity was seeking families to adopt three or four families to give gifts to, usually socks and clothing. In the first few years our family participated, my wife would buy the gifts, and our kids would help deliver them to the charity. My kids were amazed that any kids would consider socks a good Christmas gift. Socks! Our kids got new socks all the time."

By the time Tom's children were in high school, "they began spending their own money on the adopted families. They even asked us not to give them gifts because they'd rather adopt more families than get gifts of their own. My wife said, 'But we have to buy them something!' I said we didn't, and one Christmas we stuck with that."

His oldest is now 25, and "our kids still participate in the Christmas adoptions," Tom adds.

Tom's family belongs to numerous organizations and frequently participates in fundraisers. He urges his children to "leave these places better than you found them." He's also told his children that he and his wife plan to donate the bulk of their money to charity.

Still, Tom admits, "we don't demonstrate as much community involvement as we should."

Janine Harris was raised in a household of luxury, where her every material want was satisfied, often before she'd even formulated the desire. Janine knew she'd never have to earn a living. Though she might have ended up spoiled and selfish, her parents' philanthropic tendencies tempered their overindulgences.

"My Dad worked very hard and contributed major efforts and resources to the community," Janine recalls. "I saw him going to meetings and spearheading community projects. My mother volunteered, too, with the local hospital, hosting fundraiser card parties and donating to other causes."

> *"For rich children, it'd be very easy and convenient never to take any steps to build an identity outside of your association with your family's wealth."*
>
> – Jamie Johnson, director, Born Rich

"When I was growing up, all my friends were wealthy," she continues. "I didn't realize that some people had less money until I was in eighth grade. When it came time to design and order class rings, I heard one girl say she 'didn't want' the ring. ... The principal took me aside and told me the girl's family didn't have the money for luxuries. I was shocked, because I hadn't realized that she was attending the school on a scholarship, that her parents couldn't afford the tuition. The principal asked me to have the class chip in and buy a ring for the girl."

From then on, Janine "would go out of my way to make others comfortable who had less money." She relished every opportunity to excel at fundraising and other service projects.

"I did work hard in my father's businesses, ... but because I didn't need the money and because my mother preferred it, I did a lot of volunteering. I was the head of student government in high school, and I was determined to raise the most money and deliver a record number of Thanksgiving baskets to the needy."

When Janine attended college in a nearby city, she discovered abruptly how much she missed her father's connections.

"In my home city, people were eager to give my father discounts and donations. (But once) I didn't have those connections, I discovered how important they were to me," she recalls. "But I managed anyway:

I set a goal like a driven woman and pounded the pavement, just like my Dad. I was like a bull, and I always got the job done."

Years later – as a married mother – Janine found a way to give the ultimate gift: Parenting an unwanted, abused child. She had seen a documentary on mixed-race Asian boat children and, though already blessed with three beautiful children, she talked her husband into adopting another – a 5-year-old Vietnamese girl who turned out to have serious behavioral problems.

"We didn't speak her language, which was just one of many things that made the adjustment difficult," Janine says. "She was wild; she threw tantrums and shoplifted. Our three other kids were embarrassed to be around her."

"We eventually learned that Phuong had been abused by her mother," Janine says. "After a lot of counseling and tears, she finally came around. By high school, she was working a job, making good friends and starting to be responsible. Today she's a wonderful adult, with kids of her own" and a part-time job working with troubled children.

Like Janine Harris, Ellen and Laura Robinson recall very early lessons in giving back.

"Starting in first grade," Laura says, "we were always expected to serve, be involved in activities at school. ... Dad and Mom were very active in numerous local causes, and we tagged along to fundraising and appreciation events."

The Robinsons also were strongly influenced by their grandparents' generosity.

"Our grandmother taught us about servant leadership," Ellen says. "The more people feel cared about, she said, the more they want to help others and give credit to others."

These days, with their own small children, the Robinson sisters are teaching philanthropy. "Our kids have piggy banks, and they know that every dollar must be split in thirds – for saving, for spending and for giving," Ellen says.

Philanthropic adviser Charles W. Collier advises introducing children to philanthropy when they're in grade school. In the teen years, parents should take them on site visits and involve them in evaluating gift decisions. By their college years, he suggests children may be ready to join the board of the family's philanthropic fund.

But despite the family tradition of philanthropy, the Robinsons admit that they weren't always comfortable with their wealth.

"At first we tried to run away from our privilege," Laura says. "Then we realized we had an obligation to embrace it and give back. It was helpful to have our Dad's perspective: He asked us, 'What good can you do with your privilege? Donate financial gifts? Provide good jobs to the employees of our family business?' It's a major responsibility."

Community involvement is also a family affair for Karen Cosgrove Sanders.

"Tim and I are very active volunteers," Karen says, "and our kids are used to seeing that. We're involved in about a dozen boards each, and our kids hear those discussions at dinnertime."

"When we've hosted community events at our house, our kids have served food and chatted or eavesdropped. At committee meetings, my daughter – 12 or 13 at the time – would pull up a chair and chime in. (Today,) she's very excited about city issues. She likes attending public hearings and networking with political leaders and other adults."

Karen also learned recently that her college-age son had made a generous – and anonymous – donation to a community organization.

Where do all of these altruistic impulses come from?

Though they didn't volunteer alongside their parents nor do they necessarily support the same causes, "our daughters inherited our generosity," Jeff Cosgrove says. Over many years, his children saw him and Ann contributing to church committees, Rotary, a hospital, a community foundation and a suburban school that "saves the lives" of urban kids by "retraining them to be respectful."

Childhood was different for Harry O'Brian. "Volunteering was not a big part of our family when I was growing up," he says. "Mom helped at school, but Dad was working pretty hard. Our family did some giving back, but I didn't see a big emphasis."

With his own children, however, outreach is very important. Through the church they joined a few years ago, Harry's son has traveled to the developing world several times to perform mission work. "(At times,) he can be very selfish and materialistic," Harry admits, "but he still understands that giving back is an important part of his faith."

Harry and his wife are both active in community organizations, and they've encouraged their children to volunteer as well. Through the Fresh Air Fund, the O'Brians five times have hosted a mixed-race boy from New York City. "DeJuan is our kids' only serious exposure to people who aren't well-off."

"Our kids sometimes donate money of their own," Harry says. "They have a compassionate spot, more than we did growing up. They seem to know they're pretty well off and should share it."

For unknown reasons, however, the philanthropy passion doesn't always take hold.

Dan Wilson and his wife are avid volunteers – focusing most of their time, money and attention around athletics, inner-city children, arts groups and the disabled. Thanks to his flourishing business, Dan was able to establish a family foundation and has tried to involve his two adult children.

> *"When adolescents perform services for others who are less well off, they realize that they possess the capacity to do something meaningful, and by extension they learn they can live meaningful lives ... . They begin to mature into responsible adults."*
>
> – Gallo and Gallo, Silver Spoon Kids

His daughter showed early signs of philanthropic tendencies, heading up environmental and animal-rights causes at school, Dan says, and she shares those inclinations with the next generation. "When her children have birthdays, my daughter requests gifts for charities or inner-city programs," he says.

Yet her own brother, Dan's son, doesn't seem to find much satisfaction in donating or doing volunteer work. Nor does he pursue a compelling career. Dan questions whether exposure to easy money too early in his life spoiled his son's motivation to find his own purpose.

Dan now contends that society would be better off if each generation had to start from scratch, working hard to build up assets, rather than living off the wealth that their parents or grandparents accumulated.

"I believe that each person has an obligation to actualize his potential, and to use that potential fully to serve society and/or to create a business that generates employment," Dan says. "Just spending money on one's personal benefit isn't what we're here for."

> *"Giving advantaged kids chances to help others should be as fundamental to their upbringing as enrolling them in school."*
> – Gary Buffone, Choking on the Silver Spoon

Like Dan Wilson, Janine Harris believes that serving society is one of the most important values to pass on to children. Janine advises other wealthy parents, when considering how much to leave to their children, to instead guide their children to use the money to set up a foundation or do other charitable work. Giving back "broadens people's worlds," she believes.

Harry O'Brian believes that hands-on involvement functions as an important complement to donating money.

"It worries me that more affluent people seem to be callous about the plight of those who are poorer, assuming that anyone who struggles must be at fault," he says. "The wealthier people I know give a lot of money, but they don't really appreciate poverty."

He understands the contradictions facing young people today. Having visited the developing world, "my son appreciates what real poverty is," Harry says. "But he forgets that when he sees friends getting great cars."

Ultimately, experts say that giving back may benefit the giver more than the recipient, by generating a deep sense of the giver's purpose in life.

When talking about inheritances, Paul G. Schervish of the Social Research Institute suggests saying to children, "'You could use this money for your own personal consumption, or you could give some of it away to improve society.'"

Schervish adds:

> *"If your children make the decisions themselves,*
> *you may have given them a far better legacy –*
> *(the ability to figure out for themselves) what it is*
> *that produces happiness."*

"We have to teach (children) a process of caring, through wise choices, in which they connect their material means with their spiritual intention. ... It's in making this connection ... that we find our deeper identity."

— Paul Schervish, Social Research Institute

Chapter 9
The Role of Religious Involvement

For most of the wealthy families whom I have advised over the years, connection to a church or temple has been important – providing a focus for their philanthropy and volunteerism, as well as a community that supported their family life, helped shape their children, and offered solace during times of need.

But over the last generation or so in the United States, we've seen a steady decline in attendance at religious services, if not in the number of people who consider themselves spiritual.

That left me to wonder: How much do wealthy families draw on religious traditions and communities to support their childrearing? Does a religious orientation lead one to make more socially conscious decisions about money? As demographic changes chip away at our country's religious identity, are children raised in affluence more or less likely to grow up caring, generous and engaged?

Our interviews revealed a wide variety of approaches and experiences with organized religion.

Ellen and Laura Robinson grew up in a "very Catholic" family.

"Both of our parents had attended Catholic schools," Laura says. Their father's parents, in particular, "were very religious. They taught religious education classes. And when we lived with them, we went to church daily."

While the business that their family has run for several generations does not call itself a "Catholic company," the values that their grandparents embedded in the corporate culture, the sisters say, "are very rooted in Catholicism – namely, that we get to Heaven by helping others. That was our grandparents' driving force."

"Faith is very influential in our lives," Ellen and Laura say, and they're raising their children in much the same way.

While consistent participation is important to them, Ellen adds that "our parents also taught us that you could pray anywhere, not only (as part of an) institution."

Larry Weathers also is modeling his parents' practices. "My family went to church semi-regularly, enough to get the Christian foundation, and my wife and I are raising our kids in the same style."

"A faith foundation is important," Larry says. "We pray with our kids every night, though we don't insist on church every week."

Jeff and Ann Cosgrove for decades have been devoted to their faith and their church community, worshiping regularly as well as serving on various committees.

"Church involvement contributes to quality of life," Jeff says. "Ann and I believe in servant leadership – doing more than is required or expected to meet others' needs."

> *"Religion may have a salutary effect on civil society by encouraging its members to worship, to spend time with their families, and to learn the moral lessons embedded in religious traditions."*
>
> – Robert Wuthnow, sociology professor and director, Princeton University Center for the Study of Religion

"Discipline and Christian values are important. Schools don't discipline kids today," Jeff laments, "and they have no respect for teachers or elders."

"We insisted that our daughters go to church, and they resisted sometimes," he recalls. "Lisa is now active in church but Karen is not."

Looking back, Jeff says: "I could have been a better role model, a nicer person, more holy. ... (But) kids do what they want to do. We don't influence them other than to set an example. Kids want to make

The Affluenza Antidote

their own way and assert themselves, maybe out of pride."

Karen Sanders acknowledges that she, her husband and children have "zero involvement in a faith community. It's just not a fit" – though they do enjoy intellectual discussions about spirituality at home.

The Cosgroves aren't alone in seeing their grown children set aside the religious practices in which they were raised.

"Americans are going to church less often than we did three or four decades ago," writes Robert D. Putnam, author of "Bowling Alone." "Younger generations are less involved both in religious and in secular social activities than were their predecessors at the same age."

Sociology professor Robert Wuthnow describes the forces eroding religious participation: a depletion in the ranks of volunteers, as women continue to join the paid labor force; a decline in neighborhood cohesiveness; increasing divorce; and a drop in the number of people who say they believe the Bible is literally true.

Like so many of her generation, Janine Harris observes that none of her grown children currently attends formal church services, though some of her grandchildren go to Catholic schools.

"As a kid, my family always went to Sacred Heart Church together," Janine says. "Catholicism was ingrained in me. Though I married a non-Catholic, I took our own kids to church until their teen years, and my husband came with us occasionally."

Until her parents' deaths a few years ago, Janine faithfully took them to early Mass every Sunday. Now, she says she's "church shopping" and currently attends Mass at the parish where her children went to school.

Similarly, in the Smyth family, the parents' religious involvement did not lead to a lifelong faith commitment in their adult children.

Dave Smyth, who is Jewish, echoes Jeff Cosgrove in acknowledging the limits of a parent's modeling. "My wife and I may not have been a strong religious influence," he says, "because our kids don't really go to temple now."

For the O'Brian family, however, joining a different denominational community sparked new interest in faith, for both generations.

"My siblings and I attended Catholic schools and went to church regularly until we were teens," he says. "My parents weren't strict but we did attend regularly."

But Harry and his wife left the Catholic Church a few years ago for a "mission-oriented Christian church," where Harry now volunteers. Perhaps more significant, however, is the flourishing of his college-age son's faith, which has inspired him to travel three times to the Third World on church mission trips.

In the Schuman family as well, the fire burns more brightly in at least one member of the younger generation. While all three Schuman children were baptized and received First Communion, Tina "hopped around" from church to church, and George didn't attend at all.

Since his marriage to a Catholic woman, however, son Lou has blossomed from a "somewhat" religious youth into a devout adult.

"My wife grew up more spiritually than I did," he says. "Now we attend church every week, and that's been a welcome addition to my life. My wife is a church volunteer and has attended Bible school with our son."

> *"Human beings will make enormous sacrifices if they believe themselves to be driven by a divine force. ... Religious ideals are potentially powerful sources of commitment and motivation."*
>
> – Kenneth Wald, political science professor, University of Florida

The movement of some young people back into the fold may help explain why Wuthnow sees "religious commitment in our society ... holding its own against enormous odds. So many things are working against it, and yet it's doing fairly well."

Still, it's much more common for parents to see the younger generation taking a different spiritual path, or no path at all.

Though Dan Wilson's children attended regularly when they were young, today "our son has no church activity," he says. "We drag him to Christmas services."

Dan and his wife are involved in their Lutheran church, primarily

The Affluenza Antidote

in pragmatic capacities – supporting the endowment and serving on the church council – "but it's not an overriding part of our lives. The doctrine isn't what I relate to."

Their daughter, however, maintains connection to a faith community and is raising the next generation with a religious foundation.

"Our daughter brings the grandchildren to church," Dan says. "She has strong beliefs, though not the same as mine."

Characteristic of many of his peers, Dan remains open-minded. "Any faith she likes is fine with me."

Doctrine aside, observers agree that the social benefits that religious communities offer are worth preserving. Wuthnow puts that into perspective:

> *"If you could imagine a society like ours without religion – (without) those 300,000 local congregations – we'd be in a big mess. ... Religion does help people in their communities, in their family lives, their personal lives; (it) gives them meaning (and) attachments to their neighbors ... ."*

In a public school, (students have) constitutional rights. ... The disciplinary process takes time and (can be) cumbersome and complicated. ... Students quickly learn how to play the system and can tie teachers up in knots for weeks over disciplinary matters."

– Robert Kennedy, writer,
Teaching: The Difference Between Private
and Public Schools: Discipline and Due Process

Chapter 10
Shifting Attitudes About Education

Among the societal shifts that have fueled the affluenza epidemic is the dismantling of educational institutions' mandate, particularly in public schools, to discipline and shape the character of young people.

When I played football in junior high and high school, the coaches routinely hit us in the heads, pushed us into lockers, or grabbed us by the facemasks to rein in misbehavior or to make a point. In the classroom, the nuns rapped daydreaming students on the knuckles and quieted noisemakers with the swat of a yardstick. Offenses as minor as giggling or passing notes were considered punishable. Students wearing inappropriate clothing were sent home to change. And major offenses like cheating or fighting constituted grounds for suspension or expulsion.

"Discipline promotes an atmosphere for learning."
– Robert Kennedy, Teaching: The Difference
Between Private and Public Schools

I know of no student in my era who was harmed by such physical discipline or strict rules. But I do know that plenty benefited from learning who was boss in school or on the field. Being sent to the principal's office was indeed sobering, and students knew that any discipline they received in school would pale in comparison to the punishment awaiting them at home.

And it paid off, in the classroom, in the business world and in community life.

Fast-forward a generation or two. In the name of political correctness and individual rights, we as a society have robbed teachers, coaches and administrators in public schools of meaningful power to make and enforce rules. Consider the highly visible college football coaches whose recent firings – allegedly for imposing "disciplinary measures" on their players – made news.

The very people who were feared and respected a few decades ago now keep a low profile – afraid of being sued, fired, assaulted or even killed on the job. Where parents once provided backup, today they're more likely to respond to reports of their child's disruptive, even criminal behavior with verbal abuse or threats to hire a lawyer.

Bluntly put, the inmates are running the asylum. And we have only ourselves to blame.

While our society has been busy systematically stripping schools of the tools necessary to turn out civilized young people, our families have been deteriorating. With more parents divorced and/or working long hours, grandparents living far away, religion exerting less influence, and communities fragmented and apathetic, more children are growing up with few rules or role models.

Some school systems no longer recite the Pledge of Allegiance because of sensitivity over the words "under God." But straying from this tradition only removes the acknowledgment of God's authority and, in my mind, legitimizes immorality, disrespect and lawlessness.

Is it any wonder that mass killings are taking place in schools with frightening frequency? A generation ago, an event like the shootings at Columbine High School would have been unthinkable, because no student could imagine controlling his environment so thoroughly.

One of our interviewees sees it the same way.

"Schools don't discipline kids today," Jeff Cosgrove laments, "and they have no respect for teachers or elders."

For these reasons, many of today's affluent parents cannot imagine subjecting their children to the chaos of public schooling. Many pri-

The Affluenza Antidote

vate schools remain in a better position to teach values because they retain the right to discipline and expel students.

Writer Robert Kennedy agrees. "(In private schools,) everybody knows the rules. The code of conduct spells out serious consequences for disrespecting a teacher or a classmate," he points out. "By signing the contract to attend a private school, (parents and students) agree to abide by the terms ... which include consequences for infraction of the discipline code. ... Bullying, disruptive behavior and fighting are unacceptable."

In boarding schools, in particular, teachers and administrators are free to enforce rules without interference from parents who refuse to believe their child could misbehave.

Educational Challenges Facing Wealthy Families

But choosing private schools presents another kind of problem for wealthy families. Paying a steep tuition bill doesn't guarantee a parent's commitment to the child's education. Some take little responsibility for their child's character or academic achievement, assuming the school will do it all.

We all know the stereotype: the ne'er-do-well rich kid whose parents pull strings to get him into a prestigious private school, where he's surrounded by similarly apathetic, entitled, self-destructive trust-fund babies.

But how many children of affluence truly fit that unflattering profile? At their private prep schools, my son and daughter certainly encountered students who'd been spoiled by the family fortune. But they also interacted with many others who were diligent, compassionate and down-to-earth – and who went on to enjoy personal and professional success.

Also challenging the stereotype is the reality that many elite-school students – my two included – do not come from privileged backgrounds. Many have earned their spots with talent and hard work, and are paying the bills with some combination of financial aid, loans and proceeds from part-time jobs.

In many American families of affluence, attendance at prestigious schools remains an important step in achieving or maintaining rank in society, business, academia or the professions.

Yet, in the eyes of our interviewees, education appears to be much more about attaining excellence, fulfilling one's potential, developing practical skills and seeing the wider world than keeping up with the Rockefellers. In most of the families interviewed, the students have been expected to earn some of their own college expenses.

Most important, our interviewees show that the possible paths to success in academics – and in life – are as varied as the families themselves.

Fortunately for them, our interviewees who prefer public schools have been able to choose from among the best suburban districts, minimizing the impact of the anarchy and poor academic performance that characterize so many public schools.

Weighing Public vs. Private

Even before public schools deteriorated so badly, thanks to a misguided concern over individual human rights, many wealthy families weren't considering them anyway. Dave Smyth's son attended a prestigious prep school, an Ivy League university and then private law school. Janine Harris also attended only select private schools.

In other cases, what might seem like an obvious choice turns out not to be.

Though the Robinson family easily could afford to send their children to exclusive institutions, and their parents had been educated in private schools, Ellen and Laura chose public high schools. For college, they opted to move far from the communities where their family is well-known and attended a "large, anonymous" public university in California.

Later, they returned to their hometown to earn master's degrees at private institutions.

The women attribute much of their success in business and in life to their parents' willingness to give them the latitude to chart their own courses. Their father "encouraged us to explore, sample an assortment of classes, get a broad view and figure out for ourselves" what they wanted to do for a living, Laura Robinson says.

Both now have children of their own. Though "we can afford private schools," Laura says she's concerned about the lack of diversity in exclusive schools and, for that reason, sends her young son to a public school. Ellen also expresses confidence in the public school system.

Jeff and Ann Cosgrove sent their daughters to a series of public schools, moving from district to district as the family changed homes. The Cosgroves impressed upon their daughters their belief that excellent grades generate financial rewards, and stressed that achieving internal goals was more important than satisfying others' expectations.

George and Tina Schuman also prefer public elementary and high schools. They count private schooling among the many luxuries in which today's children are swaddled.

But all public schools are not created equal. Living in the area's highest-income community, George says, showed him just how "spoiled" many children are "with way too much money."

Preferring to expose their children to a "broad cross-section of students," the Schumans moved to a neighboring town that had a less wealthy population.

Attending public school was fine with Lou Schuman. "I didn't even know much about private schools (except that they were) weak in athletics and dorky."

Later, he learned to question those biases: "In college," Lou says, "I was blown away by how many (of my fellow students) had gone to prep schools."

As for higher education, while Lou and his siblings were expected to attend college, "we were not pressured to choose certain majors or colleges." Like their parents, all three Schuman children hold advanced degrees.

Today, Lou and his wife remain committed to public schools, though they sent one son to private kindergarten for one year.

Sometimes, despite the availability of praiseworthy public education in top suburban districts, private school turns out to be a better choice for certain children.

Karen Sanders' two children sampled public school at different times, but both ended up in private schools. Her son had attended private nursery school and all-day kindergarten. But when he was ready for first grade, she and her husband "couldn't justify $10,000 for private school" when they lived in a public school district with a national reputation.

Still, problems surfaced. "He went from being outgoing and confident (in private schools) to being introverted. The class was very big, and the teacher spent all her time dealing with the rowdy kids instead of focusing on the quieter ones. I heard him say once, 'I'm in first grade, but we're doing nursery-school work.'"

It was clear, Karen says, that he preferred the structure and discipline of a private school.

"He thrived under the close attention of teachers," Karen says. "(But having the opportunity to sample public school) helped him appreciate the private school environment." He now attends a marquee private university.

Later, Karen's "outgoing and ambitious" daughter, who attended private school into her teens, "outgrew" the smaller institution and switched for one year to a public middle school, where she gained even more confidence.

But, eager to return to the interactive environment of a private school and ready for a new challenge, Karen's daughter opted to board at an exclusive high school. That too is working out well, Karen says.

In the Abercrombie family, private was the norm for the elementary- and middle-school years. But when it came time for high school, Tom and his wife allowed their children to decide – and they chose public.

Tom endorsed the move. "I wanted them to go to public schools … . I thought it would be a better experience (if they interacted with) all socioeconomic groups. … We wanted them to meet farmer kids, blue-collar kids, wealthy kids."

His oldest son chose a large public high school with a "great basketball team" but failed to distinguish himself academically. But at the small private college he attended, he earned "the best grades ever" – perhaps, Tom says, because he had matured enough to work hard.

The second child started out at a "phenomenal" parochial school but, after two years of a long commute and limited social life, transferred to her brother's high school.

"What she was learning (at the parochial school) was twice what they'd learn in public school," Tom says. "Once she transferred, she didn't have to work hard. She made lots of friends and joined lots of clubs."

The younger Abercrombie children attended public high schools as well.

Tom's oldest now works for the family business in another state and is considering pursuing an MBA, as is the oldest daughter. Aptitude testing found that both would do well in business.

The second two appear more drawn to the helping professions, Tom says. Both have teaching experience, and one babysits and works in retail.

Exposing children to diversity is a common theme among our interviewees. Harry O'Brian and his brothers had attended public elementary and high schools, and he and his wife continued that pattern for two of their three children.

While the suburb where Harry, his wife and their children live is very affluent, the school district encompasses many lower-income families.

"Some of my children's friends live in modest homes," he says. "In some families, both parents work and they're still struggling." He acknowledges, though, that his children see little racial diversity.

While one might expect every wealthy family to insist on undergraduate if not advanced degrees, such was not the case for the Weathers family. Though Larry and his parents all attended college, none earned a bachelor's degree. Only his sister earned a four-year degree, and then a master's.

"Our parents had no expectations (about what studies or careers we would pursue)," Larry says. Years earlier, Larry's father had felt pressured into joining the business, and didn't want to foist that pressure on his own children. "Our parents were always interested in asking to see if we had ideas, but they never insisted."

"My parents were open to giving me opportunities and visiting colleges," Larry says, "and they were ultimately happy that I attended the state university that my sister was attending."

Larry studied business administration, economics and math while working part-time in the family business. "My father started pulling me into the fold" while Larry was in college, and taught him the company's financials.

But with four and a half years of college under his belt, Larry still hadn't found his niche, so he took a leave of absence to work full-time in the company. His interest in returning to school waned and, when his father became ill, he knew he'd stay with the business.

Will his own children follow in their parents' academic footsteps? Larry says he and his wife plan to take the same approach as his parents did – to feed their children with information to consider, then step back and let them make their own decisions.

Dan Wilson's children attended public high schools. Both were members of Phi Beta Kappa in college, and both earned master's degrees.

"We had no expectations about what they'd study," Dan says. "They were better students than I was," but they also took lighter loads than what he experienced as a mechanical engineering major at a top university.

Janine Harris reflects on how attending exclusive schools left her feeling sheltered. In eighth grade, she remembers discovering that other students couldn't afford the tuition and were attending the school on scholarship.

At times she wished she could attend a "regular parochial school" instead of the prestigious institution that her parents insisted on.

Janine's sense of being set apart continued into college, when she arrived on campus with "a trunk full of brand-new clothes where everything matched" – and was chagrined to discover that her roommates had only "a couple of suitcases with casual clothes."

Her parents discouraged her from getting a job while in college, and she knew she was missing out on an important experience. Janine says: "I wanted to be just like everybody else, to save money and work."

Her parents' protectiveness also may have kept her from choosing the career of her dreams. Janine loved foreign languages, and briefly dreamed of majoring in Russian and becoming an interpreter in New York City. But her parents wanted her to choose a traditional woman's role and stay close to home. Janine considered social work, but her parents frowned on that field's salary limitations. They encouraged her to become a nurse and "meet a nice doctor."

She did pursue graduate studies in nursing. Later, with small children at home, she performed volunteer work and took part-time jobs in a nurse practitioner program.

The Affluenza Antidote

Unlike college classmates who had worked full-time for years, Janine says, "I never worked 20 or 30 hours a week until I was in my 40s."

Her four children, however, began working at early ages and earning their own way, and they have inherited Janine's love of education: Two have bachelor's degrees, two have master's degrees, and one has a doctorate.

Paying for College

Though most of our interviewees haven't experienced a struggle to pay for education, they emphasize the importance of teaching their children self-sufficiency – managing a budget, earning money for discretionary expenses, and applying for loans or financial aid.

Most of the children appear to have learned those lessons.

"College funds of $100,000 were available to (my sister and me) at age 18, but I didn't use it except to pay for tuition," says Larry Weathers, who worked in fast-food restaurants to earn spending money while in college.

"Because we attended state schools, we had money left over and no stipulation that we spend it on education," Larry says. He and his sister used the funds remaining in their college accounts to buy their first houses.

The Cosgrove sisters began saving for college from an early age, Jeff says, using the proceeds from their antiques-dealing hobby. They also worked during college, preparing to support themselves after graduation.

Karen Cosgrove won several thousand dollars in a lottery after college. Her parents expected that she'd use it to set herself up in Boston, where she'd landed a job. Instead, she used it to travel – and then asked her parents for money to furnish her apartment.

"We refused to help her, saying she should have used her windfall," Jeff recalls. "So she took out a bank loan."

The financial skills that Karen exhibited at that age seem to have rubbed off on her daughter, who boards at an exclusive high school. Allotted educational funds by her grandparents, Karen's daughter is rapidly depleting that account even before starting college. In order to stretch those custodial funds, however, her daughter "actively negotiated with the school to give her a merit scholarship," Karen says.

As her daughter now weighs college choices, Karen can see her tempted to bypass the most prestigious private universities in favor of those that will offer her merit aid, so she can get the most for the funds in her education account.

Karen, who believes that education is one of the few areas on which a splurge may be justified, questions the wisdom of letting her daughter act on that "financial incentive."

In any case, the Sanders children are expected to allocate their grandparents' custodial funds to tuition and room and board. For discretionary spending, the children must tap their allowances and gifts.

For their part, Jeff and Ann wonder whether subsidizing their grandchildren's and great-grandchildren's high school and college educations – which became possible once the Cosgroves achieved affluence – has been prudent. "Have we deprived our grandchildren of the opportunity to make their own way?" Jeff muses.

Likewise, Tom Abercrombie wonders whether footing the entire tuition bill for his children is the best approach. His four oldest are attending or have graduated from private institutions, and he and his wife have paid for tuition, room and board so that the children can avoid taking out loans.

But Tom reflects: "I'm not sure I like that arrangement. Maybe they should have to pay for part of it." As a college student, Tom was expected to earn his own spending money while his parents covered academic and living expenses.

"Paying for college is a tough (decision for parents to make)," Tom says. "I would have wanted them to have skin in the game. If we could do it over again, I would rather split the tab. (But) if you pay the first one's tuition, how do you do it differently for the second one?"

"If one had gotten failing grades, I'd pull the plug," Tom says, "but all of the kids have worked hard to get good grades."

Should any win a scholarship, "we'd save it for them to help buy their first house or an investment" – but not a car or luxury item. And if any opt for graduate school, he anticipates, "I may change course and get them to pay for part of it."

George and Tina Schuman also harbored some ambivalence about footing college expenses. While they agreed that college decisions were their children's to make, they disagreed on whether to pay the entire bill.

"I had thought each of our children should earn $500 toward tuition," George recalls, "but (my wife said) we should pay for them to go to school."

Says Tina: "I hadn't paid for my own education, and I didn't think our kids should have to pay for theirs. My husband disagreed but deferred to me." The Schumans covered their children's tuition, books, housing and meals.

"They did have to work to earn spending money," George acknowledges. "None had a part-time job while school was in session, but they worked summers."

Dave Smyth had no hesitation about paying for all of his children's educational expenses. And Dan Wilson "certainly could afford private colleges for our children. I felt it was a good use of my money."

Writer Robert Kennedy points out: "We parents will scrimp, save, sacrifice, work extra jobs, in short do anything we have to do to ensure that our children get the best possible education. ... Giving them a head start in life, teaching them the value of hard work – these are things that matter to most parents."

Unfortunately for the Wilson family, that willingness to "do anything" for his children has backfired. While Dan's daughter maintains a stimulating hobby business, his son went to a "playboy school" and has drifted from field to field. Perhaps because he gave them "too much money too soon," neither child has become financially independent. His daughter is going through a divorce, and, much to Dan's chagrin, his ex-son-in-law will end up with money that he intended to keep in the family.

Harry O'Brian takes a more balanced view. He expects his children to earn their own spending money while in college but not to cover tuition and room and board, as his parents had done for him and his siblings.

Harry's parents have invested in 529 plans for all of their grandchildren, "(but) my kids pay for their own nonessentials such as entertainment and travel." His son works in a restaurant during college semesters to earn spending money – a necessity he learned the hard way.

"He didn't work hard enough the previous summer, so he didn't earn enough to get him through the semester," Harry says. "I didn't bail him out (by giving him more money). It was a huge opportunity to teach him."

He continues: "They all know that they have to have careers." But, like some other affluent parents, Harry fears that his children hold an unrealistic view of adult life.

"My kids want to make a lot of money, though they don't understand what's involved. They want to live a certain lifestyle – the one they enjoy now."

> *"It's not a real job if Junior writes his own job description, comes to work whenever he feels like it, demands an exorbitant salary, and stirs up resentment among the other employees."*
>
> – Gary Buffone, Choking on the Silver Spoon

Chapter 11
The Family Business:
A Blessing or a Curse?

Much of the motivation for writing this book has sprung from my decades of work with business-owning families – and my concern for the long-term viability of those firms. The bulk of America's wealth lies with family-owned businesses, which account for 80 to 90 percent of all business enterprises in North America. Such businesses employ 62 percent of the U.S. workforce, according to the *Family Business Review*.

Family firms have long been hailed as leaders in responding to the market's needs, enriching their communities, and demonstrating long-term commitment to their employees and vendors. Research also shows that family firms tend to outperform nonfamily businesses.

Consider Anheuser-Busch Cos. Inc., which flourished for four generations until its recent sale. Enterprise Rent-a-Car continues its explosive growth under the second-generation leadership of Andrew Taylor. And many are interested to see how Fidelity Investments – still under the direction and ownership of its founder – will fare.

Unfortunately, however, the majority of family-owned businesses fail to achieve longevity. As the *Review* reports, some 30 percent survive into the second generation, while 12 percent remain viable into the third; only 3 percent of all family businesses are still operating in the fourth generation or beyond.

Throughout history, families have shown a remarkable tendency to dissipate their fortune by the third of fourth generation. Andrew

Carnegie reportedly coined "Shirtsleeves to shirtsleeves in three generations," while a Scottish proverb expresses the phenomenon another way:

> *The father buys, the son builds,*
> *the grandchild sells,*
> *and his son begs.*

Clearly, society benefits when family businesses thrive. Sadly, many are stymied by the challenge of transitioning to the next generation of leadership. While the founders pour blood, sweat and long hours into their businesses, their children often seem to lack similar passion and commitment – though they do enjoy the material comforts that their forebears' success brings them.

Observing this pattern firsthand, I noted that these younger people seemed cut from different cloth than their parents and grandparents were. Some wanted nothing to do with the family enterprise; others took the jobs that were handed to them but delivered little – generating tension among other employees and dragging down performance.

> *"Expecting (your children) to share your enthusiasm, perseverance and entrepreneurial pride in what you founded and built into a success can set you up for disappointment."*
> – Jane Adams, Ph.D., psychologist and author

Coupled with ever-intensifying foreign competition and technology demands, it's easy to see why so many family businesses end up controlled by outsiders or shut down. In either case, communities are deprived of yet another important source of cohesion, social responsibility and stable employment.

I wondered: Why did the children of such self-starting, hardworking, innovative folks turn out so apathetic and entitled?

Surely, our culture – which frequently highlights appalling behavior, glorifies celebrities, and prizes style over substance – is partly to blame. But I also wondered whether the tendency of wealthy parents to make their children's lives too comfortable was contributing to a growing scarcity of achievement.

Children in affluent families can be so accustomed to a free ride that they never learn how to work. Often, they face so many attractive opportunities that they cannot choose any.

For many, the only well-paying job they can get is with the family business – which may help account for why such enterprises often fail to thrive.

> *"No matter how motivated or how much the parents want them to take over, (the child) may simply not be capable of doing the job."*
>
> – Gary Buffone, Choking on the Silver Spoon

But, refreshingly, our conversations with interviewees showed that the once-proud tradition of passing a thriving business from parent to child *does* live on – though the families who succeed at this may be scarcer than they were in past decades.

Naturally, because we chose interviewees based on their success in managing their affluence, these families have had largely positive experiences around family businesses. Still, their attitudes toward being a business-owning family may offer some guidance for others.

I find it striking that, in several cases, the dominant influence comes from grandparents who crafted the business and continue to shape and inspire the younger generations. Consider Ellen and Laura Robinson, whose veins run with passion for the family business.

"Our family is our company," Laura says. Their grandmother, who founded the business, considered it a noble calling to provide jobs that would allow people to support their families during wartime. She believed that offering employees higher wages and caring for them in other ways would assist them in supporting both their families and their customers.

Their father followed in those footsteps, expanding employment opportunities locally and in distant communities, and raising the bar on quality and service.

Ellen began working there at age 14, and Laura still does, but they never took those opportunities for granted. Knowing that jobs in the family company awaited them, the sisters motivated themselves to prepare fully. Both worked in complementary industries to gain different perspectives, and later pursued master's degrees in business.

"Our Dad always wanted us to study what we were passionate about," Laura says. "We were lucky to find jobs that related to our family's industry so we could come back with more confidence" and fresh ideas.

She adds: "We're in business not to make money but to make a difference in people's lives. Profit is a measure of doing the right thing, not a goal in itself."

"Happiness doesn't come from wealth," Laura continues. "We have what we need; we have our reason to get up in the morning."

Like their grandmother, Laura and Ellen remain devoted to serving others. They express appreciation when they see their employees' teamwork and caring attitudes permeating the business.

Just imagine: What would our society be like if young people were exposed to more Laura Robinsons and fewer Paris Hiltons? Too many children of wealth, I've observed, seem to lack the markers of well-groundedness that Laura describes – a reason to get up in the morning and a sense of fulfillment.

Based on research, success in resisting affluenza – which tends to afflict young inheritors perhaps more than any other group – would seem to be rare.

Buffone writes:

> *"Those who inherit great fortunes, or high positions*
> *in the family business, are often left with a gnawing*
> *sense of inner doubt, wondering if they could have*
> *ever made it on their own. ... Most of the hard work,*
> *sacrifice and ability were the prior generation's,*
> *not theirs. No matter how hard they work, their*
> *accomplishments are often overshadowed."*

How did the Robinsons avoid this fate? Anyone who knows the family would see that they have long shunned materialism as a driving force, and have adopted as a family mission the responsibility to provide jobs and enhance the community's quality of life.

Like the Robinsons, Larry Weathers has inherited a passion for the family business, and has put his own mark on the enterprise.

He can't remember a time when he didn't want to work for the family firm. Long before he even understood what the company sold, "I put my father on a pedestal and wanted to do what he did."

Because Larry's father had felt pressured to join the business, his parents were determined not to repeat that mistake with their children. They avoided talking shop at home – but that didn't dampen young Larry's interest. He loved traveling with his father to industry conferences, which showed him "both the business and personal side of my father."

And he was eager to prove himself. As a high-schooler, "I did grunt work (in the business) and froze my tail off. I learned the inventory and got to know all the employees. ... My Dad was pleased to have me work there. I didn't have to apply for a job, but I didn't get any special treatment because I was the owner's son."

Larry attended college but never found his niche at school. He decided to take a leave of absence to work full-time. When his father became seriously ill, he knew he'd stay at the company. Larry is now president, and his mother is CEO; his sister and wife work there as well.

"My wife was very motivated in college, (earning a) teaching certificate and a master's in education," Larry says. "But then she fell in love with the business."

Like their father, Larry's young children say they want to work where their Dad works. One small son insists he and his wife will work together, as his parents do and grandparents did. Larry says with amusement: "He doesn't know that not all couples share an office."

Lou Schuman also has made a career in the family business. But the job was not handed to him; he had earned an engineering degree and an MBA, and worked for several other companies before returning home.

That education and outside experience, Lou says, helped him see the need to "rightsize" the company and to eliminate absentee shareholders. That involved buying out his two siblings, both of whom had worked briefly for the business before choosing other careers.

George Schuman avoided promising his children jobs in the family firm. He expected them to gain experience and develop skills in other places.

"After college, our oldest wanted to join the family business," George says, "but I asked him to wait five years" and acquire relevant skills elsewhere. Taking a few years to further mature and gain a well-rounded perspective also helps.

The experts support George's reasoning. Buffone notes: "The successor needs to learn to deal with both the headaches and responsibilities of various positions in the business and to work harmoniously with the employees."

Observers also advise parents to realize that the business may hold different emotional meaning for their children than it does for them. Psychologist Jane Adams writes:

> *"(Children may see the business) as a rival for*
> *parental attention. They often view it as an*
> *expression of someone else's vision, not their own.*
> *It may require different skills and talents*
> *than they have or want to acquire. ...*
> *It might not be a business or profession that*
> *personally compels their interest."*

Growing up around family enterprises gave Janine Harris early and realistic glimpses into day-to-day business operations. Her father ran a variety of companies, several of which she worked in. She never had to go out and find a job, she acknowledges, but neither did she get a free pass.

"I got to work at 6 a.m. and worked hard," Janine says.

Instilling a similar passion for work and sense of accomplishment in the next generation has been important to her.

"I reminded (my children) that they'd always have to pay their bills," she says. Today, one of her children works in an enterprise launched by Janine's husband.

Jeff Cosgrove and his brother grew up with a family firm but chose not to work there. Today, having founded several companies of their own, Jeff says they're happy to have one daughter and two grandsons working with them.

For the O'Brian children, family-firm ownership didn't occur until they were adults; the two generations bought a company that parents and children could run together. Two of the children remain with the business today, and their father is part-time chairman.

For some families, though, succession doesn't proceed as planned. Though Dan Wilson's children saw his business "develop from scratch," neither ended up making it their career.

"Initially my son identified with me and joined the company," Dan says. "He started out with a good work ethic." But the two clashed in their views on the business, and Dan's son left.

Observers suggest bracing oneself for such an eventuality.

"Like all kids, your adult children may fail to live up to your expectations, at least some of the time," writes Jane Adams of the Family Business Institute. "They may not share your vision, your energy, your standards or your smarts."

Dan adds: "My son (went on to earn) his MBA and became a stock trader. He lost a lot of the money I gave him, but my company keeps replenishing him."

Once it became clear that neither of his children would run the company, and he had earned enough to retire on, Dan arranged for his employees to buy the firm.

"I haven't taken a salary since I was 60," Dan says. "I don't need the money." Recently, he helped his wife and daughter launch a business venture.

Experience has convinced Dan that no family should be allowed to endow its children with great wealth. Believing fervently that younger generations are better off if they are forced to make it on their own, he plans to leave the bulk of his estate to charity.

Nor does Tom Abercrombie expect to bequeath the family firm to his children.

"I really struggled with the question of my children joining the family business," Tom says. "Do I want to hand them a job and career? ... Having five kids forced me to think about these things. What if all five and their spouses were here working? We need to be fair to each one; we can't let one in and the next one not."

He has seen children join a family business because it's convenient and then never really pull their weight. He's also seen businesses tear families apart.

"A consultant I know who has 500 family-business clients admitted that none were happy," Tom says. "His whole business is based on how to restructure the family business to make the family happier."

"I don't want to give (my children) a place to settle; it would be too likely to make them unhappy," he believes. "If they worked in the business, they might fight with each other. (If they stay out of the business) I'll have a better personal relationship with the kids, and the kids with one another."

> *"Nothing could be closer to heaven on earth when you have your kids in business with you and everything is going well – and nothing is closer to hell on earth when you have your kids in the family business and things are going badly."*
> – Don Schwerzler, founder, Family Business Institute

To prevent such problems, Tom and his wife have decided to allow their children to join the family business after college only temporarily. Tom wants to help them learn as much as possible – and then move on to something else.

That policy is good for the business, he believes. Without his children on board long-term, "(our company) can hire much more talented people because they know they have a shot at the top spot. And the upper management guys are really willing to help my son (who's worked at the company temporarily), because he'll never be competition for them."

My own observations – and those of the experts – back up Tom's concerns. Family businesses make too many hiring decisions based on emotion – trying to shield their children from life's painful lessons – rather than business sense.

Gary Buffone has observed: "A family hires a lazy son-in-law because otherwise he'll be unable to support their daughter. A father hires his

The Affluenza Antidote

son for an executive position ... because he can't find a job elsewhere. Parents offer their daughter a job ... to keep her from taking their grandchildren and moving to another state."

Keeping his children out of the company also will allow Tom to retire without complications. "I'd like the option to sell my business without having to worry about saving it for my kids."

He also wouldn't want his children to take over the business for the benefit of their parents. "I would rather see my kids make their own decisions about how to spend their money."

He advises his children: "Do what you enjoy, not what has been laid in your lap." He has offered to help finance businesses or other endeavors that his children decide to pursue.

Says Tom: "I would rather have a happy family than an unhappy family business."

Part III

"Parenting has changed dramatically over the last two generations. The Great Depression and World War II shaped our grandparents' experiences. By contrast, increases in postwar productivity sparked a period of unprecedented affluence, and the majority of the baby boom generation grew into adolescence, taking financial security for granted.

"Parents have more disposable income and offer their children considerably more than the basic needs of food, clothing, shelter and medical care.

"... Children have become the central focus of American life, and many more children are growing up in millionaire households. However, lavishing money and material goods on children can disrupt children's healthy development. A parent's best intentions may lead to an erosion of their children's work ethic, indulging them in the name of love or skewing priorities by focusing only on opportunities and privileges."

– BMO Financial Group,
Raising Healthy Children in Families of Affluence

Conclusion
Can We Reverse Course?

The trends are irrefutable and disheartening: Technology and the media dominate every corner of our lives, instilling in even the youngest children a ravenous appetite for material goods. Religious and civic communities exert less influence. In educational systems, individual rights too often trump societal benefits.

But the most discouraging trend of all may be the erosion of family life as the bulwark against a cold, uncertain, dangerous world.

Where a strong home environment once bolstered an individual's ability to hold his own and thrive in a tough environment, too many of today's children are growing up without that foundation.

Divorce is taking its toll, as is the movement of both parents into the workforce. Families eat together less often. Frequent job changes and relocations splinter extended families, depriving children of a sense of identity and continuity. Children spend more time in organized activities and less time in creative, exploratory play. Computer games, Facebook and iPods crowd out family conversation and interaction.

Sadly, we parents have ourselves to blame for most of these developments. In an effort to give our children *everything*, we have deprived them of a great deal. As the number of wealthy American families has risen, so has the deterioration of family life. People may have more material comforts today, but those comforts haven't brought greater happiness, engagement or a sense of identity.

Surely this is not what our parents and grandparents envisioned.

With the singular goal of creating a better life for their children, they endured hardships to come to this country, and worked long hours in their businesses, on their farms or in factories. Where the teaching of bedrock values was once a given, many of today's children are simply failing to learn respect, self-sufficiency, compassion and an appreciation for opportunities

And our entire society is suffering for it.

Common Traits of the Affluenza-Resistant

As discouraging as these trends may be, it's important to recognize those rare families who are determined to strengthen their children's resistance to the debilitating effects of affluenza.

While every family is unique – and no one can identify or control all of the factors that generate success – we did find some common ground among our respondents. Specifically, the interviews showed that children of affluence tended to benefit from the following, which mitigate the impact of uncontrollable factors:

▉ **Strong family role models, particularly grandparents, who were steeped in Depression-era values.** Regular contact with extended family tends to reinforce the value systems of earlier generations. Some families go to great lengths to cultivate those relationships, traveling thousands of miles to vacation together. Others have moved from out of state in order to be close.

▉ **A commitment to carving out family time.** Interacting together frequently – whether for meals, house and yard work, school assignments, old-fashioned fun, or vacations – provides precious opportunities to get to know one another, to nourish a child's identity and worth, to generate long-term security, and to pass along values. The more face time available to a family, the more likely the children will absorb the messages that parents strive to instill.

▉ **The role of a prosperous family business in instilling a work ethic in younger generations, and in keeping those young people close to home.** While the majority of family businesses do not endure, the successful ones often provide an impressive venue for propagating values, and offer extraordinary opportunities – but only for motivated, well-prepared children.

▓ **A healthy respect for money and hard work,** and an awareness that pursuing an engaging occupation and achieving one's goals are vital to well-being.

▓ **Emphasis on philanthropy, volunteerism and job creation.** In almost every case, respondent families demonstrated a strong commitment to the welfare of others and worked to instill a social conscience in succeeding generations.

▓ **Detachment from the urge to keep up with the Gettys.** Several interviewee families showed a resolve to buck societal trends, shunning video games, excess consumption and exclusive association with high-income people.

▓ **A willingness to let children find their own way, take responsibility for themselves and learn life's sometimes-painful lessons.** Most of our interviewees allowed their children to make their own choices regarding college and career.

▓ **An expectation that educational systems and faith communities can do only so much**, and that the buck stops with the family to provide solid grounding.

One Expert's Suggestions

Others have observed additional common denominators that may help a family develop well-adjusted, successful children. Based on his research, author and wealth counselor John L. Levy highlights several traits and practices that characterize families with healthy attitudes toward wealth:

▓ Parents who are comfortable, clear and balanced about their wealth and where it came from, and who talk with their children constructively and honestly about the family's fortune.

▓ Families that emphasize social responsibility, philanthropy and prudent spending.

▓ Estate planning that keeps inheritors informed well before the death of a parent.

▓ Transfer of wealth while parents are still living, often in stages, but only to children who demonstrate financial maturity.

■ Refusal to pressure a child to deny his or her true nature in order to claim an inheritance.

■ The setting of good examples by both parents; the demonstration of ample love, counsel, listening and encouragement to endure; and support for children to cope with frustration and disappointment.

■ A recognition that not all children can or should be treated equally. Levy says that those who have no interest in the family business, for example, should not be given the same number of shares as children who will devote their working lives to the company.

■ Insistence that the child choose and commit to work that is meaningful to him or her, whether inside or outside the company, and whether lucrative or not.

■ Encouragement of personal and/or spiritual development.

■ Encouragement of friendships with people who are not resentful, envious or exploitative – people whose lives are full enough that they need not flatter or manipulate a wealthy friend.

■ Opportunities for inheritors to prove to themselves that they don't need the family money to lead successful lives.

No Magic Bullets

Of course, there's no foolproof recipe for success. DNA and birth order strongly influence children's personalities. Much remains unknown about risk factors for alcoholism, substance abuse, mental illness and depression. As well, the death or disability of a parent often can traumatize a child.

While many would argue otherwise, our interviewees' experiences suggest that neither religious affiliation nor the type of education chosen influence children's well-being as strongly as does the dynamic of the family itself.

But even the most diligent families will find that heeding others' experiences and advice won't guarantee a happy, successful junior generation.

As well as our interviewee families have done, none is perfect. Many admit to questioning some aspects of their own upbringing, and they recognize their own mistakes – many of which grew out of confusion, inexperience and societal pressures.

What these families do offer us is an antidote to the destructive messages that our society delivers nearly 24/7 – messages that fuel Americans' addiction to consumption and an aversion to hard work and responsibility. To be sure, external influences can never be eliminated. But our interviewees have shown that well-considered guidance can mitigate affluenza's most destructive effects.

A Final Word

For wealthy parents who are obsessed with appearances, or who simply can't bear to see their children struggle to earn what they desire, the suggestions and experiences outlined here are likely to fall flat. After all, parents who are not themselves grounded, focused on building something of value, and cognizant of the larger world cannot pass along a commitment to tenacity, self-sacrifice and the value of an honest day's labor.

Parents who are patient, mature and well-rounded enough to give their children room to identify and explore their own passions, free of the taint of excessive familial wealth, have a better chance of seeing the next generation – and our society – reach its full potential.

New York Times columnist Thomas Friedman offers reason to be hopeful:

> *"Our parents truly were the Greatest Generation.*
> *(We) have been what the writer Kurt Andersen*
> *called 'The Grasshopper Generation,' eating through*
> *the prosperity that was bequeathed*
> *us like hungry locusts.*
>
> *"Now we and our kids together need to be*
> *'The Regeneration' – the generation that renews,*
> *refreshes, re-energizes and rebuilds America*
> *for the 21st century."*

References

Introduction

Danko, William, and Stanley, Thomas. *The Millionaire Next Door: The Surprising Secrets of America's Wealthy*. Longstreet Press, 1996.

Chapter 1

U.S. Bureau of Labor Statistics.

Peace Parenting Project. http://www.peaceparenting.org/index.htm

Gibbs, Nancy. "The Magic of the Family Meal." *TIME Magazine*, June 4, 2006 (citing Robin Fox, Rutgers University)

Schlosser, Eric. *Fast Food Nation: The Dark Side of the All-American Meal*. Houghton Mifflin, 2001.

National Marriage Project, Rutgers University. http://marriage.rutgers.edu

Robbins, James. "The Costs of Rising Divorce Rates Across the U.S." *EzineArticles.com*, February 22, 2008. http://ezinearticles.com/?The-Costs-of-Rising-Divorce-Rates-Across-The-US&id=1003126

Solomon, Christopher. "The Swelling McMansion Backlash." MSN Real Estate, 2009. http://realestate.msn.com/article.

aspx?cp-documentid=13107733

Centers for Disease Control and Prevention/
National Center for Health Statistics, 2009.
http://www.cdc.gov/nchs/fastats/overwt.htm

U.S. Department of Health and Human Services, Office of the
Surgeon General. http://www.surgeongeneral.gov/topics/obesity/
calltoaction/fact_adolescents. hml

Putnam, Robert. *Bowling Alone: The Collapse and Revival of
American Community.* Simon and Schuster, 2000.

Seligman, Martin. "Life Matters," Radio National, 2002.
http://www.abc.net.au/rn/talks/lm/stories/s648530.htm

2002 American Family Business Survey, MassMutual/Raymond
Family Business Institute, 2002.

Astrachan, Joseph, ed. *Family Business Review*, Family Firm
Institute Inc.

Chapter 2

Sahadi, Jeanne. "Millionaire Households at Record."
CNNMoney.com, April 30, 2007. http://money.cnn.com/
2007/04/30/pf/millionaire_counties/index.htm

Senior, Jennifer. "Rich Kid Syndrome," *New York Magazine,*
January 7, 2008.

Buffone, Gary. *Choking on the Silver Spoon: Keeping Your Kids
Healthy, Wealthy and Wise in a Land of Plenty.*
Simplon Press, 2003.

Brooks, David. "The Sandra Bullock Trade," *The New York Times.*
March 30, 2010.

Baker, Dan. *What Happy People Know: How the New Science of
Happiness Can Change Your Life for the Better.* Rodale
Press, 2003.

Boodman, Sandra. "Sick of Expectations," *The Washington Post.*

August 1, 2006. (citing Madeline Levine, *The Price of Privilege*)

Boodman, Sandra. "Sick of Expectations," *The Washington Post.* August 1, 2006.

Levy, John. *Inherited Wealth: Opportunities and Dilemmas.* BookSurge Publishing, 2008.

Hausner, Lee. *Children of Paradise: Successful Parenting for Prosperous Families.* Tarcher; 1st edition, 1990.

Le Van, Gerald. *Raising Rich Kids.* Xlibris Corporation, 2003.

Astrachan, Joseph, ed. *Family Business Review*, Family Firm Institute Inc.

Raising Healthy Children in Families of Affluence: Meeting the Unexpected Challenges of Wealth. Harris MyCFO Inc., BMO Financial Group, 2007.

Chapter 4

Gibbs, Nancy. "The Magic of the Family Meal." *TIME Magazine,* June 4, 2006.

Gibbs, Nancy. "The Magic of the Family Meal." *TIME Magazine,* June 4, 2006. (citing Robin Fox, Rutgers University, and Miriam Weinstein, *The Surprising Power of Family Meals*)

National Center on Addiction and Substance Abuse http://www.casacolumbia.org/templates/Home.aspx?article id=287&zoneid=32

Chapter 5

Collier, Charles. *Wealth in Families; second edition.* Harvard, 2006.

Collier, Charles. *Wealth in Families; second edition.* Harvard, 2006. (citing Lee Hausner, *Children of Paradise*)

Buffone, Gary. *Choking on the Silver Spoon: Keeping Your Kids Healthy, Wealthy and Wise in a Land of Plenty.*

Simplon Press, 2003.

Le Van, Gerald. *Raising Rich Kids.* Xlibris Corporation, 2003.

Goldsmith, Barton. "Raising Children in Affluent Families," 2002.
http://www.emotionalfitness.net/articles/affluent.htm

Boodman, Sandra. "Sick of Expectations," *The Washington Post.*
August 1, 2006. (citing Madeline Levine, *The Price of Privilege)*

Chapter 6

Kristof, Nicholas. "How to Lick a Slug," *The New York Times.*
August 1, 2009.

Louv, Richard. *Last Child in the Woods: Saving Our Children from
Nature-Deficit Disorder.* Algonquin Books, 2005.

Buffone, Gary. *Choking on the Silver Spoon: Keeping Your Kids
Healthy, Wealthy and Wise in a Land of Plenty.*
Simplon Press, 2003.

Le Van, Gerald. *Raising Rich Kids.* Xlibris Corporation, 2003.

Chapter 7

Buffone, Gary. *Choking on the Silver Spoon: Keeping Your Kids
Healthy, Wealthy and Wise in a Land of Plenty.*
Simplon Press, 2003.

Collier, Charles. *Wealth in Families; second edition.*
Harvard, 2006. (citing Kathryn McCarthy, Rockefeller
& Company)

*Raising Healthy Children in Families of Affluence: Meeting the
Unexpected Challenges of Wealth.* Harris MyCFO Inc.,
BMO Financial Group, 2007.

Tomlin, Robyn. "Extended-Family Living Suits Us Just Fine,"
StarNewsOnline.com, 2009. (citing John Graham, University
of California/Irvine)

Chapter 8

Gallo, Eileen, and Gallo, Jon. *Silver Spoon Kids: How Successful Parents Raise Responsible Children.* McGraw Hill, 2002.

Le Van, Gerald. *Raising Rich Kids.* Xlibris Corporation, 2003.

Senior, Jennifer. "Rich Kid Syndrome," *New York Magazine,* January 7, 2008. (quoting Jamie Johnson, "Born Rich")

Collier, Charles. *Wealth in Families; second edition.* Harvard, 2006.

Collier, Charles. *Wealth in Families; second edition.* Harvard, 2006. (citing Paul Schervish, Social Research Institute)

Buffone, Gary. *Choking on the Silver Spoon: Keeping Your Kids Healthy, Wealthy and Wise in a Land of Plenty.* Simplon Press, 2003.

Chapter 9

Collier, Charles. *Wealth in Families; second edition.* Harvard, 2006. (citing Paul Schervish, Social Research Institute)

Putnam, Robert. *Bowling Alone: The Collapse and Revival of American Community.* Simon and Schuster, 2000. (citing Robert Wuthnow, Princeton University, and Kenneth Wald, University of Florida)

Abernethy, Bob. *Religion & Ethics Newsweekly,* episode no. 534. Public Broadcasting System, April 26, 2002. (citing Robert Wuthnow, Princeton University)

Chapter 10

Kennedy, Robert. "Teaching: The Difference Between Private and Public Schools: Discipline and Due Process," About.com Guide to Private Schools. http://privateschool.about.com/od/choosing aschool/qt/comparison.htm

Chapter 11

Astrachan, Joseph, ed. *Family Business Review,* Family Firm Institute Inc.

Adams, Jane. "Parenting Adult Children," Family Business Institute. http://www.family-business-experts.com/parenting-adult-children.html

Buffone, Gary. *Choking on the Silver Spoon: Keeping Your Kids Healthy, Wealthy and Wise in a Land of Plenty.* Simplon Press, 2003.

Schwerzler, Don. "Parenting Adult Children," Family Business Institute. http://www.family-business-experts.com/parenting-adult-children.html

Conclusion

Raising Healthy Children in Families of Affluence: Meeting the Unexpected Challenges of Wealth. Harris MyCFO Inc., BMO Financial Group, 2007.

Levy, John. *Inherited Wealth: Opportunities and Dilemmas.* BookSurge Publishing, 2008.

Friedman, Thomas. "The Fat Lady Has Sung." *The New York Times,* February 20, 2010.

About the Author

Veteran wealth manager James V. D'Amico was the first president and CEO of Genesee Valley Trust Company, founded in 1994 in Rochester, New York. Under D'Amico's leadership, the privately owned Genesee Valley Trust – which advises some of Western New York's most prominent, successful businesses, families and charitable organizations – had grown to manage $618 million in assets by 2007.

Genesee Valley Trust was acquired in January 2008 by the publicly held Canandaigua National Bank & Trust Company. D'Amico remained president and CEO at Genesee Valley Trust until retiring in June 2009.

For more than 10 years, D'Amico wrote a regular column, "Managing Wealth," for the *Rochester Business Journal.* From 2007 to 2009, he also wrote the column, "Real Benefits," for *The Journal of Compensation and Benefits.*

Active in the community, D'Amico served on the boards of the Rochester Philharmonic Orchestra, the Rochester Area Community Foundation, the Legal Aid Society, and the Rochester chapter of the American Heart Association. He was a volunteer solicitor for Heritage Christian Services and the Al Sigl Community of Agencies.

Though they maintain ties to Rochester, D'Amico and his wife now live in Sarasota, Florida, near two of their children and three of their grandchildren. In addition to spending time and vacationing with his family, D'Amico enjoys golf, tennis, reading, oil painting and bridge. He welcomes readers' comments at jd@AffluenzaAntidote.com.

Made in the USA
Lexington, KY
22 September 2011